God Never Forgets

God Never Forgets

Faith, Hope, and
Alzheimer's Disease

DONALD K. McKIM, EDITOR

Westminster John Knox Press
Louisville, Kentucky

Scripture quotations from the New Revised Standard Version
of the Bible are copyright © 1989 by the Division of Christian Education
of the National Council of the Churches of Christ in the U.S.A.
and are used by permission.

Grateful acknowledgment is made to the following:
Tyndale House Publishers, Inc. for permission to quote from Robert Davis,
My Journey into Alzheimer's Disease, © 1989. All rights reserved.

Little, Brown and Company for permission
to reprint the poem by Emily Dickinson in chapter 6,
ed. Thomas H. Johnson, *The Complete Poems of Emily Dickinson*
(Boston: Little, Brown & Co., 1960).

Orbis Books for permission to reprint the poem
by Emilie Townes in chapter 2. From Emilie Townes, ed.,
A Troubling in My Soul: Womanist Perspectives on Evil and Suffering
(Maryknoll, N.Y.: Orbis Books, 1993).

Book design by Jennifer K. Cox
Cover design by Pam Poll
Cover image © 1997 PhotoDisc, Inc.

First Edition
Published by Westminster John Knox Press
Louisville, Kentucky

This book is printed on acid-free paper that meets the
American National Standards Institute Z39.48 standard. ♾

PRINTED IN THE UNITED STATES OF AMERICA

97 98 99 00 01 02 03 04 05 06 — 10 9 8 7 6 5 4 3 2 1

Library of Congress Cataloging-in-Publication Data

God never forgets : faith, hope, and Alzheimer's disease / Donald K.
McKim, editor. — 1st ed.
  p.   cm.
Proceedings of a conference held Oct. 10–12, 1994, at Memphis
Theological Seminary.
  Includes bibliographical references and index.
  ISBN 0-664-25704-6
  1. Alzheimer's disease—Religious aspects—Christianity—
Congresses.   2. Alzheimer's disease—Patients—Religious life-
Congresses.   3. Alzheimer's disease—Patients—Family
relationships—Congresses.   I. McKim, Donald K.
BT732.G63   1997
259'.4196831—dc21   97-25541

CONTENTS

v

93919

FOREWORD

Alzheimer's disease is becoming increasingly visible as a frightening and debilitating illness. The announcement that former President Ronald Reagan is now a person with Alzheimer's disease has brought this condition into the national consciousness with particular poignancy. Its degenerative nature and the deterioration of a person's mental capacities—particularly the memory—make it a disease in which physical life is sustained while mental faculties are lost.

The prominence of this disease and its attack on human memory raise crucial theological questions. It will become increasingly important for the Christian church, its theologians, and its laity to consider Alzheimer's disease in relation to Christian understandings of the human person, God, and what the church believes about God's grace, salvation, and life eternal. These issues must be addressed both for the sake of those who become persons with Alzheimer's disease and for those who are their caregivers. David Keck has named Alzheimer's the "Theological Disease." He writes:

> This disease does differ from other examples of disease, anguish, and death. The unusual situation of a prolonged mental deterioration and the need for sustained caregiving over many years means that we can no longer presume the existence of the cognitive subject when we are thinking theologically. The loss of

Foreword

memory entails a loss of self, and we can no longer be secure in our notions of "self-fulfillment." Indeed, our entire sense of personhood and human purpose is challenged. Because we are dealing with the apparent disintegration of a human being—indeed the apparent dissolutions of many, many human beings— a thorough reconsideration of many fundamental theological questions is not entirely out of order.[1]

The wholesale devastation Alzheimer's disease brings leads Keck to call it "Deconstruction Incarnate"—the self seems to be dissolved.[2] Surely addressing a problem of this gravity is a must for the Christian church.

On October 10–12, 1994, Memphis Theological Seminary hosted a conference to help in these tasks. "Memory and Hope: Alzheimer's Disease in Biblical and Theological Perspectives" brought together speakers from several theological disciplines to explore theological issues raised by Alzheimer's disease. This conference was made possible through the Virgil H. and Irene R. Todd Lectureship at the seminary as well as by a generous grant from the H. W. Durham Foundation of Memphis. Various forms of assistance were also received from the Alzheimer's Association–Memphis Area Chapter through the work of the director, Dr. T. Wright Pillow, and the Alzheimer's Day Services of Memphis.

Plenary speakers for this event were Dr. James W. Ellor, Dr. Denise Dombkowski Hopkins, and Dr. Stephen Sapp. Their presentations focused on biblical, theological, and pastoral care dimensions of Alzheimer's disease. We are pleased to make these important addresses available now to a larger audience through this book. We are grateful to the speakers for graciously providing their materials for this project.

This book is dedicated to all persons who suffer from Alzheimer's disease and to all their caregivers and loved

---

1. David Keck, *Forgetting Whose We Are: Alzheimer's Disease and the Love of God* (Nashville: Abingdon Press, 1996), 15.
2. See the title of Keck's chapter 1.

Foreword

ones. It is offered with the prayer of the apostle Paul: "May the God of hope fill you with all joy and peace in believing, so that you may abound in hope by the power of the Holy Spirit" (Rom. 15:13).

Donald K. McKim
Memphis Theological Seminary

CONTRIBUTORS

James W. Ellor is Associate Professor of Human Services at National-Louis University in Wheaton, Illinois.

Denise Dombkowski Hopkins is Professor of Hebrew Bible and Director of the Doctor of Ministry Program at Wesley Theological Seminary in Washington, D.C.

Stephen Sapp is Associate Professor of Religious Studies at the University of Miami in Miami, Florida.

Editor

Donald K. McKim is Academic Dean and Professor of Theology at Memphis Theological Seminary in Memphis, Tennessee.

1
Celebrating the Human Spirit

JAMES W. ELLOR

*M*rs. Smith and Mr. Jones live on the frontier of reality, relationships, and the richness of the life that they have known and understood since birth. Mrs. Smith and Mr. Jones have Alzheimer's disease. This uncharted terrain offers them things that seem vaguely familiar and things that are completely foreign. Mrs. Smith and Mr. Jones do not understand this space. Their families and friends do not understand it either. It involves loss of memory, loss of the ability to reason, and, as the disease progresses, loss of intelligible speech. Someone who loses a foot has a visible loss that becomes the focus of both rehabilitation and support for that person and his or her family. Those who have lost their memory are generally misunderstood. They are often alienated from their peer group and even family members. Few diseases cause so much anxiety as the loss of memory through Alzheimer's or a related cognitive disorder causes among older adults and those who care for them.

Alzheimer's disease currently affects approximately four million people. Estimates suggest that this figure will climb to fourteen million in the next fifty years. Most church congregations know of at least one and often several families who have been touched by this devastating infirmity. This terminal illness was discovered by Alois Alzheimer in 1904. At present, it is challenging to diagnose accurately, and it is progressive and irreversible. Alzheimer's disease strikes at what in Western society is considered to be the heart of the nature of the person.

Alzheimer patients cling to as much of their identity as possible, given the nature of this illness, which reduces both memory and logic functions in the brain. In the early stages the person often demonstrates personality rigidity that was not previously in evidence and may become reclusive. As the elements of memory, personality, and the ability to think things through rationally slip away, the person needs fellow travelers who can share the journey, offer guidance along the road, and eventually become a new container for his or her sense of self, dignity, and transcendence with the world.

The role of the pastor and religious congregation is to be that fellow traveler. At times we are needed to support the person with Alzheimer's, particularly in the early phases of the disease. At other times we need to be there for the patient's family, and at times we need to offer that same support for ourselves. Watching someone that we care about go through the phases of Alzheimer's disease is a constant process of anticipatory grief and loss. Often this journey takes everyone involved into uncharted terrain. As with any journey, if we allow the anxieties of the journey and our human desire to arrive at our destination to dominate our thinking, the process becomes a burden and we can even wish the individual with Alzheimer's disease dead. Yet if we can see the journey as a part of life, our goal can become the reflection of God's love. From this perspective we can better see the impaired person as one who has strengths and weaknesses, and we can become a fellow traveler through the last days of his or her life. This can be challenging: as the person with Alzheimer's goes through the phases of the disease, he or she may be difficult to love, and our own grief may be heavy to bear.

In this chapter, the focus will be on understanding the needs of those who have Alzheimer's disease. We will discuss how the impact of the disease on the patient affects our understanding of the person in theological and wholistic terms.

The Impact of Alzheimer's Disease

The human spirit is at once a source of who we are as persons—our creativity, our uniqueness, our self-transcendent abilities—and at the same time reflective of our finite nature as persons living in God's world. This spirit does not leave the person who contracts Alzheimer's disease. However, our skills for understanding the psyche and spiritual aspect of the person must find new forms of expression in order to perform our ministry functions.

Most of us, especially those of us who are in ministry, do not realize how dependent on the ability to communicate and on memory we are until we encounter a person with a profound cognitive impairment. Our skills for listening, for helping a person to gain insight into his or her life's experiences, our basic ability to understand the faith of the older adult are all based on cognitive abilities that are weakened in and ultimately lost by the person with Alzheimer's disease. Caregivers and members of the community of faith need to learn new skills for support of this special group of God's children.

Memory

Throughout life, human beings create memories. Our earliest memories are often of our nuclear families, school, friends, and favorite playtime activities. Throughout adulthood, we are shaped by our partners in life, the development of our own families, our friends, as well as all the events and activities both within and outside the home that are important in our maturing sense of self. Many seniors have noted that much of their self-concept seems to be contained in the person that they have been. Someone who is eighty years old clearly has more to remember than a younger person. All these things become the history of the person. They are locked up in memory. The memories that make up our self-image are actually perceptions of events and stories of the various activities and relationships that we have had. They are not *objective realities* in the sense that they are carefully videotaped and recorded by *objective* sources. Rather, our sense of who we are is colored by a combination of our experience of reality, the perceptions of those around us who also experience these moments, and the memories of these events. If the person has struggled with any type of substance abuse, some of these memories may also be affected by the chemical response to memory that is consistent with the substance.

When the average person wishes to recall the story of her life, she will call on her memories of the narrative along with those of the people around her. Memory plays a critical role, both in terms of placing us in the ongoing story of our lives and even in terms of how others perceive us. When we meet a friend, part of what makes that person a friend is the history of our relationship. If a friend begins to forget the people whom he or she has cared about, the friendship often becomes strained. This can also be said for family members. Children, even adult children, seem to want their parents to be custodians of their own early childhood memories as well as the recognition of who they are today. Most people don't stop to think how integral are memories—their own memories and the memory of others—to their own self-concept.

Memories are contained by more than the individual. They are shared with those we care about, as well as contained in the records, photographs, and other memorabilia that we accumulate. These people and things tell the story of who we are and what we have been about in our lives. Often, as persons grow older, they move their memorabilia from the home they lived in with their children to one that is smaller during retirement, and one that is still smaller in their later years. Thus progressively fewer of the *things* that offer visual cues of memory continue to be available to them.

Theologically, the nature of the person is less dependent on human memory than we might think. The nature of the person as created by God is in relationship with God. Who we are as a person is in relation ship with God, with other people, with ourselves. Human memory plays a part in this relationship for human beings, but not necessarily for God. Process theologians point out that memory offers a way of keeping track of the relationships between past and present. Based on these memories, we create the expectation of our future. When the memories of the past are interrupted or impaired by Alzheimer's disease, too often people presume that all relationships with the past, with fellow human beings, and with the future are also impaired. However, if we examine this from the perspective of our relationship with God, the cognitive impairment is seen as less important. God has not forgotten. Indeed, if friends and family continue to support the person with Alzheimer's, then they have not forgotten either. In these cases other sources of memory can take over the impaired functions of the physical memory of the person with the impairment in much the same way as an artificial leg can take over many of the functions of a person's own leg.

Memory is a source of communication, both in terms of the recognition of the relationships one has with other persons and in the related functions of the brain and speech. As Alzheimer's disease progresses, the ability to speak complete sentences is progressively impaired. Observation of speech patterns suggests that the person will begin by *forgetting* most proper nouns and then begin to lose track of all nouns. Eventually, the person's speech will become laden with adverbs and adjectives, and finally it will be reduced to little more than clauses. In the most advanced stages of the disease, speech is often unintelligible to all but those who know the patient best, and then the intuition of the caregiver comes more into play than verbal communication. Thus, memory as a way of telling the story is impaired when the person becomes forgetful. And when the speech center, which is also a function of the human brain, is also impaired, communication is further hampered, even the communication of basic human needs.

James W. Ellor

Theological Considerations

Critical to this discussion is the answer to the question, Where is the soul of the person who has Alzheimer's disease? If the person who has Alzheimer's disease is somehow separated from his or her soul, then many traditional philosophers and theologians would say that the person regresses to a lower life form. But if the person is not in some way separated from his or her soul, then he or she is still a person, with the potential to be in relationship with God. This latter position is taken by most theologians. The person is still a person, albeit impaired of memory.

The problem theologically is determining what role memory plays in the nature of the "self" or "personhood" of the individual. This question is one that has also been addressed in psychology for many years. In 1949, Gardner Murphy, in his classic *Historical Introduction to Modern Psychology,* posed the issue as follows:

> While primitive cultures differ as much in their psychology as they do in their basketry and pottery, or their kinship systems, they show a general preoccupation with one recurrent problem—the nature and attributes of the soul. The dramatic difference between a sleeping and a waking person invites the thought that something has gone out and then returned. The awakening person may recount a battle in which he or she took part while, manifestly, his or her body lay still upon the ground. In illness, especially in delirium or coma, something seems to disappear which may, upon recovery, reappear. The conception of a psychic entity—detachable soul, we may say—makes sense.[1]

The implication for the ancient Greeks, as noted by Murphy, or for the family member or nurse's aid who works with a person with Alzheimer's disease, is the notion that the body can be alive while the essence of what makes the person a person can separate from the body. If that which makes the person a human being—someone like you and me—is lost, then the body that is left is no longer a part of a real person and can be treated as one sees fit. This type of duality, or splitting of body and soul, is consistent with post-Socratic Greek philosophy, but not with the Christian message. The older adult is a person with a soul. That means that he or she is a person. If he or she is a person, then he or she should be treated with the same respect one would direct toward any other person. The task for bridging theology and psychology is to articulate a theological basis for employing psychology to address these questions. In this case, one aspect of theology, a theological view of human nature, may offer such a bridge.

Calvin

Many theological positions can be called upon in discussing the soul. We find one that is helpful for this discussion in the writing of John Calvin (1509–1564). While he lived three hundred and fifty years before the discovery of Alzheimer's disease, his thought on the nature of the soul and when it departs the body is a part of the orthodox Reformed theological tradition and is similar to the thinking of many other Protestant theologians.

Calvin believed that human beings are composed of a body and a soul. He defined the term "soul" as "an immortal yet created essence, which is our nobler part. Sometimes it is called 'spirit.'"[2] Calvin goes on to say that when "the word 'spirit' is used by itself, it means the same thing as soul; as when Solomon, speaking of death, says that then 'the spirit returns to God who gave it.' . . . When the soul is freed from the prison house of the body, God is its perpetual guardian." This soul, according to Calvin, is "endowed with essence." The human mind is endowed with preeminent gifts that testify to the immortal essence. Calvin goes on to note that human beings are superior to animals. He makes this argument with the statement: "But the nimbleness of the human mind in searching out heaven and earth and the secrets of nature, and when all ages have been compassed by its understanding and memory, in arranging each thing in its proper order, and in inferring future events from past, clearly shows that there lies hidden in man something separate from the body."[3] In short, the soul is endowed with some small reflection of the mind of Adam before the Fall. Calvin notes that the conscience is the sign of the immortal spirit. This soul is a separate essence from the body. Finally, the soul leaves the house of clay (the body) at death.

Calvin notes that humans were created in God's image. He makes the distinction between the outer person and the inner person or soul. Calvin notes that while the outer person reflects God's glory, the soul is the "seat of his image."[4] It is this image that raises humanity above all other creatures. Mary Potter Engel notes:

> Calvin, both here and elsewhere, uses the *imago Dei* model to interpret the microcosm model. Thus, for Calvin to say that humankind is a microcosm means that the human being is a preeminent specimen of *God's* wisdom, power, and justice. . . . It is a microcosm because, as the specially chosen image of God, humankind as a whole is the showplace and recipient of God's wonders and gracious benefits.[5]

Critical for our discussion of persons with Alzheimer's disease is our understanding of the soul and reason. Clearly Calvin understands that the soul is the reflection of God in humanity. It is this soul that makes the person human, therefore above animals. However, it is also the ability to reason which sets us apart from lower life forms. Since the soul does not leave the earthen vessel until death, then persons with Alzheimer's disease are persons with a soul. However, since reason and will, as Calvin would have understood them, are diminished and subsequently lost prior to death, it is clear that Alzheimer's patients are in some ways diminished as persons. Calvin is assured that the person has reason. However, he never seems to address how persons of impaired intellect fit in with the remainder of humanity. One can only speculate that the emphasis for Calvin is on the presence of the soul, and therefore, all the discussions later in the text as to how we are to treat one another would apply. Calvin clearly states: "We should infer from this that man is made to conform to God, not by an inflowing of substance, but by the grace and power of the Spirit."[6] If it is not by our doing, but by grace that we come to God, then it should be possible for even the Alzheimer patient to do so!

The role of the soul is critical in the thinking of Calvin. For Calvin, the soul is the eternal reflection of God in humanity. It is the soul, aided by reason, will, and understanding that allows the individual to see God as reflected in the Word. Calvin clearly understood that the soul comes to God at the point of death.

Calvin also had a respect for the nature of the person. He understood that each person has a soul, which is what sets him or her above the lower species. The person is a reflection of God and therefore deserves the respect of all fellow human beings.

In many ways it is easier to take a theological position that Mrs. Smith or Mr. Jones has a soul and should be respected than it is to utilize the current ministry tools to understand the nature of the soul as a part of the person as offered by the pastoral literature. Religious congregations, clergy, and lay leaders are generally restricted to cognitive means of knowing or understanding the faith of another person. If a person of any age is asked, "Are you a religious person?" or "Tell me about your faith?" the response will incorporate the intellectual symbols or terms of that person's faith tradition, for example, "I am Presbyterian" or "I believe in God." If the person simply says yes or no, or just turns away and walks off, it is difficult to know about her or his spiritual "self." However, this may be the response of a person with a middle or advanced stage of Alzheimer's disease. The Alzheimer condition teaches us how heavily the average pastor or lay leader depends on cognition to understand the spiritual nature of friends and neighbors.

Pastoral Considerations

Working with someone who has Alzheimer's disease begins with understanding the nature of the condition. This disease is only one of more than one hundred and fifty possible causes of the symptoms of confusion and memory loss. Even such basic medical conditions as an asymptomatic urinary tract infection can cause a disturbance in memory among older adults. Obtaining the proper diagnosis is important. Medical conditions that *are* reversible can manifest symptoms similar to those of Alzheimer's disease. With these conditions the symptoms of memory loss and confusion go away with proper treatment. What follows here will assume that Alzheimer's disease has been diagnosed.

Stages of the Disease

Alzheimer's disease develops slowly over time. Some causes of confusion and memory loss can have a sudden onset, but this is not the case for Alzheimer's disease,[7] which is a progressive, degenerative, terminal illness. If there is no other disease, a person can live for more than five years with this condition. Diseases of lifestyle, such as ulcers or even high blood pressure, can even improve when a person contracts Alzheimer's disease. This is because the person experiences not only memory loss but less stress as he or she reaches the more advanced stages, and stress can be a cause of these lifestyle-related disorders.

Cognitive disorders like Alzheimer's disease affect the entire functioning of the brain. From the perspective of the nonmedical practitioner this means that both memory functions and the ability to use rational thinking are impaired. When theologians like Paul Tillich talk about the nature of the self, implied is each person's ability to express that nature. Alzheimer's disease follows a progression of cognitive debilitation that can be traced in stages. As the stages progress, the person slowly loses his or her ability to think through even the simplest tasks in everyday living. The affected senior is unable to talk about his or her faith or to express the nature of the self. He or she is even unable to say "Thank you for visiting."

Several observers of Alzheimer's disease patients have offered *stage theories* to track the progression of this disease. Like most stage theories, there are problems intrinsic to the methodology. Defining actual stages is useful, but finding definitive criteria to delineate the movement between stages is often difficult. Further, the question of regression is also problematic. Most Alzheimer's disease patients have "good" days and "bad" days. Does this transition reflect regression of stages, idiomatic changes, or environmental changes?

One useful stage theory, offered by the Portland Chapter of the Alzheimer's Disease Association, defines four phases. (See Figure 1.) This theory offers insights as to cognitive, functional, and personality changes for each phase.

As the disease begins to take hold, the person with Alzheimer's employs basic coping patterns to combat this threat to what psychodynamic therapists would refer to as "ego functioning." The person struggles to maintain his or her sense of self and may not be able to face the fact that something is wrong. Unfortunately, it is in this early phase that friends and members of the congregation may reject the person as being "stubborn" or "a pain to be with." If a clergyperson or lay leader is told that the person has Alzheimer's disease, many react by wanting to remove that person from positions of responsibility in the congregation. During this early stage, and into phase 2 as described in Figure 1, the person may have difficulty with memory and logic functions, but he or she continues to have feelings and a need to be needed and to "fit in" the community. In churches we may need to add supports for the person in order to protect the functions of the congregation. For example, if the impaired person is the treasurer of a class, club, or the congregation, he or she may need an assistant treasurer who understands the situation and makes sure the books are properly kept. The person with Alzheimer's should *not* be abruptly removed from positions that are sources of emotional gratification and support.

It is important to understand that the person who has Alzheimer's disease, throughout the course of the disease, *has feelings*. Too often, particularly in the latter stages or phases of the disease, the person is talked about as if he or she is not present or treated like a child. It has become socially acceptable in

Fig. 1. Phases of Alzheimer's Disease
(Summary)

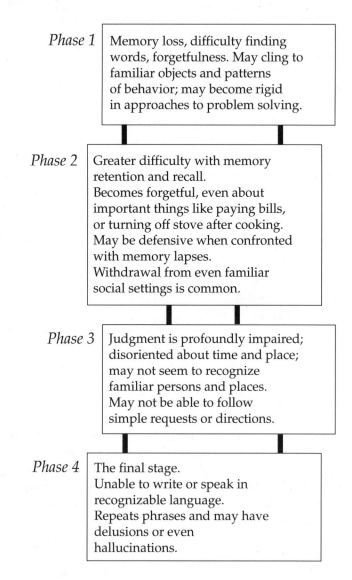

Phase 1 | Memory loss, difficulty finding words, forgetfulness. May cling to familiar objects and patterns of behavior; may become rigid in approaches to problem solving.

Phase 2 | Greater difficulty with memory retention and recall.
Becomes forgetful, even about important things like paying bills, or turning off stove after cooking.
May be defensive when confronted with memory lapses.
Withdrawal from even familiar social settings is common.

Phase 3 | Judgment is profoundly impaired; disoriented about time and place; may not seem to recognize familiar persons and places.
May not be able to follow simple requests or directions.

Phase 4 | The final stage.
Unable to write or speak in recognizable language.
Repeats phrases and may have delusions or even hallucinations.

Source: Portland Chapter of the Alzheimer's Disease and Related Disorders Society.

some institutional settings to treat Alzheimer's disease patients if they are some type of lower life form or a body without a soul, as discussed earlier. It bears repeating: the person who has Alzheimer's disease still has feelings. He or she may not be able to respond to or process these feelings. Thus as the disease progresses we see progressively more primitive coping mechanisms employed to address anxiety or adversity. One rule of thumb is to treat those with Alzheimer's disease the way you would want to be treated!

In the final stages of the disease, the person with Alzheimer's may have to be placed in an institution, even though family members are reluctant to do so. When a caregiver is jeopardizing her or his own health, the help of full-time health care professionals is necessary. Many long-term care facilities have special units that are designed specifically to accommodate the needs of persons with Alzheimer's disease.

Working with Persons Who Have Alzheimer's Disease

Numerous books offer specific techniques for working with persons who are cognitively impaired. Here I will summarize some basics. The first principle of working with a person who has Alzheimer's disease involves a value, rather than a technique. A person who has this disease is still a person. This person should be valued as a person, albeit a person who has memory loss. As memory and reason become progressively impaired, in a sense, the person will slowly become unable to be the carrier of his or her own memories or story. Thus, it becomes the role of those who care about the person to do so. Functionally, the role of historian and memory keeper will usually be picked up by a spouse or family member. But a minister or other lay caregiver can also become a fellow traveler, helping to share the story.

A second principle concerns memory loss. If loss of memory is suspected, be sure that the person is seen by a physician. Too often we assume that *all older adults normally lose some memory*.

This negative stereotype is unfounded. The only correlation between aging and memory is in terms of the speed of memory. With age, it may take a bit longer to remember and to recall important things. This is often not noticeable for either the individual or their friends.

A diagnosis may indicate that some intervention is needed. In the church, we should try to keep persons in the early stages of Alzheimer's disease involved in the various aspects of the life of the congregation to which they are accustomed to being a part. Concerned persons can provide memory cues, such as a shopping list or a "to do" list. The problem with a shopping list is that it can be lost. Establishing a single place where it is always kept may reduce the frequency of losing the list. Establishing other routines concerning personal hygiene and eating can also be helpful. Such routines are more likely to be successful when they are based on routines the Alzheimer's patient was familiar with before the onset of the disease.

When modifications in church routine to accommodate a person with Alzheimer's disease will affect other persons, impacted by these modifications, how many people should be told that Mr. Jones or Mrs. Smith has the disease? On the one hand, if the congregation is to help, at least some members need to know what the problem is. As persons of faith, we may not know to pray for the impaired individual if we don't understand the problem. However, it may not be necessary to make a general announcement to the entire congregation. Most people with Alzheimer's do not want people to be told, or to notice that they have a cognitive impairment. As with most major illnesses, insensitive people will isolate the person, or say things that are awkward at best. The very forces of healing that can be found in a congregation, because we are a people of God, can turn destructive when they are employed by persons responding from fear or their own anxiety and ignorance.

Those who do know that someone has Alzheimer's disease may find the following tips helpful for interacting with that person:

Celebrating the Human Spirit

Begin by gaining the attention of the impaired person. Often those who have Alzheimer's disease, particularly those who are in the later phases of the disease, are distracted. They may not notice your attempt to talk with them until you gain their attention. Often an appropriate touch on the arm, or if the person is sitting, getting down to his or her level to be able to make eye contact is helpful.

Speak with the person in a manner in which you would want to be addressed. Because of stereotypes of persons with memory loss, many people talk down to Alzheimer's-impaired people. At times, the impaired person may actually seem more aware of what you are feeling than you are. While the impaired person may not be able to fully process the implications of your behavior, he or she will feel it and react to it.

Try to make any request for action by the impaired person simple. Remember that he is both impaired in memory and in logic. Thus something as simple as signing a name may be too complex. It would be more appropriate to ask him or to take a piece of paper, then take the pen, then move his hand to the line, then to write his name on the line. This type of breaking down the task is difficult to do without talking down. However, if done with respect, it is possible. Note that the more advanced the disease, the smaller the steps into which the task should be broken.

As noted above, cognitively impaired people still need self-esteem. Try not to treat them in ways that take this away. Try to find things that they can do that allow them to continue to feel needed.

Remember that the lives of family members often

become as disrupted as that of the impaired person—and sometimes even more disrupted. Care and concern for caregivers as well as support for them is critical for their ongoing ability to cope with this difficult disease.

One topic that is often neglected in the literature on working with persons who have Alzheimer's disease is that of meeting their spiritual needs. Those who have Alzheimer's disease are not able to express their faith or even their gratitude to someone who visits them to talk about their faith. Those in the more advanced stages of the disease may not find traditional worship services meaningful. They may even be disruptive. A congregation that does not seem to mind the disruption of a small child may seem to resent disruptions by a cognitively impaired older adult. Too often impaired persons in the more advanced stages are incontinent; they might soil the carpet or pew at a chapel or meeting place. Such impairments should not become excuses for keeping the senior from attending worship. Adaptations to worship can be made to allow the impaired senior to participate. For example, J. W. Ellor, J. Stettner, and H. Spath have developed an approach to worship for cognitively impaired people.[8] Experience has shown that family members who worship with cognitively impaired persons can find a bond that was thought to be lost.

Churches should develop other methods of supporting the spiritual needs of cognitively impaired members. Those in the early phases of the disease should be encouraged to participate in all their accustomed sacred rituals and activities. As the person moves through the phases, he or she needs encouragement to continue, possibly in adapted rituals that meet his or her needs. Those in the advanced phases should not be exposed to traumatic images, such as scripture passages about a person being stoned to death or battles. Such images reflect trauma that may frighten a cognitively impaired person and cause disruptive behavior. Beyond adapting traditional rituals, creative new rituals should be developed that are consistent with the impaired person's religious beliefs and tradition.

All the activities of faith noted above should be offered in a manner consistent with those beliefs the person held prior to the onset of the disease. These are the rituals that the person will identify with and will be most able to participate in. Since the person is cognitively impaired, I would argue that he or she must not be pushed to give up former beliefs and convert to a new way of thinking, because this violates the historical dignity of the impaired person.

Advocacy

An important role for the pastor and lay leader who deals with cognitively impaired people is that of advocate. As suggested earlier, the first place for advocacy is in ensuring that the impaired person has proper diagnosis of the disease. However, as impaired people become progressively less in command of their own world, they need someone to walk with them, someone who will look out for their needs and interests, perhaps in ways their caretakers cannot do. James W. Ellor and Robert B. Coates suggest that this type of advocacy reflects three levels of response (see Figure 2).[9] The most obvious is *case advocacy.* Case advocacy has previously been referred to as

> **Fig. 2. Levels of Advocacy**
>
> Case Advocacy
> Community Advocacy
> Class Advocacy

supporting the person and his or her family. Making sure that appropriate diagnosis and medical care are available as well as supporting the person's right to be treated as *a person* is also a part of this.

Community advocacy becomes important when it is clear that the problems and concerns of a cognitively impaired person are shared by other residents of the local geographic or congregational community. For example, the creation of a caregiver support group is a form of community advocacy that brings together people with similar needs and concerns. The development of an adult day-care center specifically designed for cognitively impaired individuals is an example of this level of concern.

Class advocacy is the third level. When clergy and lay leaders all over the country realize that a class of persons—for example, the class of all persons who have Alzheimer's disease—needs help, and pursue the concerns and needs of this group, they engage in class advocacy. Class advocacy supports the common needs of a specific group of persons with some type of common identity across communities at state, national, and even international levels. The Alzheimer Disease Foundation is one group that engages in this type of advocacy. Its work generates money for research on Alzheimer's disease and for programs at national and state levels.

Another type of advocacy involves coordinating the work of the religious congregation with that of other human service and medical agencies serving an Alzheimer's patient. Separation-of-church-and-state stipulations are often cited as the reason why human service agencies fail to include religious groups as a part of the caregiving network. However, nothing prevents congregations from reaching out to the human service agencies to compare their work and coordinate efforts. This is particularly important in such areas as home health and counseling. For example, if the church is providing rides or encouraging the impaired person to get out of the home for a walk, the church should check with the home health agency, where applicable, to be sure that these activities are appropriate. The medical professionals might prefer that the congregation engage in other activities that have not been considered by the church.

Continued Recognition
of the Whole Person

The role of memory in the nature of the self seems to reflect its capacity to contain the history of the person. Where there is not memory, there is no perceived history. For persons with Alzheimer's disease, only the external sources of their history can be maintained. Yet, without this sense of history, it is common for such persons to find other indicators of health improve. As the memory is lost, so is the stress of daily living that most of us experience and convert into ulcers, high blood pressure, and colitis. Perhaps at the root of this improved health is a lack of caring: the Alzheimer's patient in the second or third stage of the disease ceases to care about social pressures or social norms. Indeed, except for occasional spurts of insight and memory, the ability to experience themselves as self-transcendent persons is generally lost. Ministry with persons suffering this type of loss requires a wholistic approach.

Wholism, or wholistic approaches to pastoral care, are defined in many different ways. Often the distinguishing feature is not *physical, social, emotional,* or *spiritual* but rather how these various elements interact or combine. However this is understood, most of us can agree that the human spirit is difficult to isolate, but it is that which permeates all aspects of the whole person. Often the spiritual aspect serves the role of integration, bringing the various aspects of the self together. With the breakdown of cognitive ability, it is difficult, but *not* impossible, to reach out to the spiritual aspect of the person. Recognition of the role of the cognitive aspect allows the pastoral counselor to emphasize the affective and behavioral aspects of his or her ministry. Music, poetry, repetitive activities, and human interaction are all important aspects of this type of work. While creativity may be called for in ministry to those with loss of cognitive ability, giving up should not be considered an option. Those in the beginning stages of Alzheimer's disease continue to need to feel that they are a part of, and cared about by, the congregation and clergy.

People affected by Alzheimer's disease continue to impact the world around them. They require someone to care for and about them. When they live with a spouse or an adult child, these caregivers need to be considered a part of any ministry; when they live in an institution, the institution staff as well as the family should be a part of the ministry. Ministry also needs to be integrated with the work of the local social service agencies that are concerned about the older adult.

James W. Ellor

If an older adult needs an amputation of a leg, the world knows how to respond. We help replace the lost mobility with crutches, an artificial leg, or other alternative ambulatory devices. When a person is losing memory and cognition, we need to do similar things: find ways to use alternatives to memory and rational thinking. These people continue to be persons with souls. They are still members of the faith community. They call us to be creative in our ministry in ways that other members of the congregation do not require. This is an important challenge, not a burden.

Failing Brain, Faithful God

DENISE DOMBKOWSKI HOPKINS

*a*n article in the *Washington Post* two years ago detailed the case of "Baby K," born with anencephaly, a congenital defect in which a major portion of the brain, skull, and scalp is missing.[1] Stephanie, as her mother called her, could not see, hear, or think. Her mother battled legally to force Fairfax Hospital in Virginia to keep Stephanie alive whenever she ran into breathing difficulty, which happened more than six times. The case went all the way to the Supreme Court; meanwhile Stephanie reached her second birthday. Most of the one thousand children like her born each year live only about a week. Stephanie died last year at age three.

What has the case of "Baby K" to do with exploring Alzheimer's disease in biblical perspective? A great deal. For Stephanie's mother anchored her reponse to Stephanie's condition in her reading of the Bible. Despite the assessment of the hospital, the American Academy of Pediatrics, and countless medical ethicists that there existed no treatment that could help Stephanie live to think or feel, her mother believed that her daughter would be normal one day. Others have been healed, why not she? "In my darkest, darkest moments," she said, "I read my Bible and stand on God's word." Belonging to a prayer group led by John Hagee, a San Antonio minister with a national TV show, Stephanie's mother played Hagee's tape, "Healing Scriptures," during her daily visits to the hospital. Hagee insists, "Where there's life, there's hope. Nothing is impossible with God."

Would such a belief in miraculous healing be a message of hope for persons with Alzheimer's disease and their caregivers or a cruel hoax? Alzheimer's is a progressive, degenerative disease that attacks the brain and results in impaired memory, thinking, and behavior for an estimated four million Americans. In its final, terminal stage, victims become totally incapable of caring for themselves. There is no cure for this disease, which robs people of their memory, identity, and relationships. Alzheimer's is the most common form of dementing illness. More than one hundred thousand people die of Alzheimer's every year, which makes it the fourth leading cause of death in adults, after heart disease, cancer, and stroke.[2]

The "Baby K" case points up how the Bible can cut like a double-edged sword in the struggle with Alzheimer's disease. The Bible does not provide easy, or sometimes even helpful, answers for the questions raised by Alzheimer's disease in the way that a bumper sticker I saw suggests: "Find help FAST . . . in the Bible pages." There are no quick fixes in the Bible, just as there are no quick fixes in the treatment of Alzheimer's. Stephanie's mother's insistence upon miraculous healing makes clear the inescapable fact that the Bible does contain passages that can be dangerous and damaging in the battle with Alzheimer's disease. An uncritical use of the Bible to explain the suffering of Alzheimer's or to hold out false hopes can place additional burdens on already-burdened patients and caregivers.

Rebecca Chopp argues in her foreword to a remarkable book by Nancy Eiesland, *The Disabled God: Toward a Liberatory Theology of Disability*, that biblical teachings "allow either one of two options for those with disabilities [and I would add, for those with chronic or progressive diseases like Alzheimer's]: miraculous healing or heroic suffering."[3] Neither option models an appropriate or helpful pastoral/congregational response to

Failing Brain, Faithful God

Alzheimer's disease. As many feminist theologians have long argued, biblical texts are not always prescriptive. Sometimes they are descriptive, mirroring human sin and cultural norms rather than what God intends for us.[4] Texts articulating the two options identified by Chopp, miraculous healing and heroic suffering, often function descriptively rather than prescriptively when it comes to dealing with Alzheimer's disease.

The biblical record has shaped Judeo-Christian and cultural attitudes toward disease and disability, helping to marginalize and isolate victims and their caregivers, especially when healing does not come or suffering is not borne heroically. Robert Davis experienced the impact of these attitudes in his own struggle with Alzheimer's disease. Davis, the former pastor of the largest Presbyterian church in Miami, was diagnosed with Alzheimer's disease in 1987 at age fifty-three. In his autobiography, *My Journey into Alzheimer's Disease: A True Story*, he asks: "How many Christians are loaded down by well-meaning children, friends, and care-givers who sincerely feel that by their spiritual exhortations they can force Christ to penetrate into their loved one's troubled mind? All they are doing is unwittingly convincing them that they have perhaps somehow in their loss with reality committed the unpardonable sin, or else that they are truly cut off and forsaken by God."[5]

In fact, the Bible shows the arbitrariness of God when it comes to healing and disease, an arbitrariness that pushes us to questions of theodicy. Disease comes as punishment from God to the Israelites who make the golden calf (Ex. 32:35), as an inexplicable test from God of Job's faith and endurance (Job 1 and 2), or as a means of letting the Egyptians know through the plagues that Israel's God is Lord (Ex. 7:4–5). In the healing stories of the Hebrew Bible, Elijah in 1 Kings 17 revives from death the son of the widow of Zarephath, a foreign woman who does not worship the God of Israel. His successor Elisha heals Naaman, commander of the Aramite army, of his leprosy (2 Kings 5) and revives the son of the Shunammite woman (2 Kings 4).

Healing comes to these foreigners but is denied the innocent baby boy who is the product of King David's illicit union with

Denise Dombkowski Hopkins

Bathsheba, despite David's urgent fasting and repentance (2 Samuel 12). Good King Hezekiah is healed from near death by God (2 Kings 20), yet poor King Saul, who is caught in the difficult transition between the period of the Judges and the monarchy, is tormented by mental illness caused by the evil spirit of the Lord until he commits suicide in battle (1 Sam. 16:14; chapter 31). God sends disease or healing for different divine purposes, in seemingly capricious ways. Jesus heals some people of blindness, leprosy, or hemorrhages in the Gospels, but he does not heal every disabled person he meets. Indeed, David Blumenthal goes so far as to speak of the necessity of acknowledging "the awful truth of God's abusing behavior" and facing it with "a theology of protest and sustained suspicion" in this "post-Holocaust, abuse-sensitive world" of ours.[6]

The penitential laments in the book of Psalms acknowledge sin as the cause of present suffering in mind and body. For example, "there is no soundness in my flesh because of your [God's] indignation; there is no health in my bones because of my sin" (Ps. 38:3; see also Pss. 6; 32; 51; 102; 130; 143). This confession acknowledges disease as divine punishment for sin and also functions as a motivation for God to act and change the psalmist's situation—that is, to heal. Often, the psalmist's suffering is compounded by the taunts of enemies who equate the psalmist's suffering with God's punishment and God's deliverance with healing, as in Psalm 22:8. On the other hand, angry laments protest that the psalmist has done nothing to deserve the present suffering, as in the self-curse of Psalm 7: "O LORD my God, . . . if there is wrong in my hands, . . . then let the enemy pursue and overtake me, trample my life to the ground" (vv. 3, 5).

Some biblical texts, like the purity codes, equate perfect bodies with spiritual wholeness and service of God, implicitly underscoring the link between disease/disability and sin, as well as implying the need for repentance. Leviticus 21:17–23, for example, prohibits anyone from drawing near to God to offer food in sacrifice "who has a blemish . . . who is blind or lame, or one who has a mutilated face or a limb too long, or one who

Failing Brain, Faithful God

has a broken foot or a broken hand, or a hunchback, or a dwarf, or a man with a blemish in his eyes or an itching disease or scabs or crushed testicles." Blemished—that is, sinful—priests violate God's holiness.

Lest we think that this linkage between sin and sickness is confined primarily to the Hebrew Bible (what Christians call the Old Testament), we need only to look at Hebrews 9:14, which carries forward the exclusionary thinking of Leviticus 21 by proclaiming a Christ who "offered himself without blemish to God," echoing the view throughout Leviticus 17—26 that those who represent God must be perfect. In Hebrews 7:26, the unblemished priest becomes a type or model of Christ, the "high priest, holy, blameless, undefiled, separated from sinners and exalted." In Ephesians 5:27, Christ is the Lamb "without a spot or wrinkle or anything of the kind . . . without blemish." These texts become dangerous when they are used to measure all humanity against a standard of perfection in mind and body. The result can be despair for people with Alzheimer's disease and their caregivers. It can seem that their repentance is not sincere enough to warrant healing, or even that their sin, that is, their illness or disability, disqualifies them from repentance and healing altogether.

In Luke 5:18–26, a paralyzed man is lowered down through the roof on his bed by his friends into the middle of the crowd surrounding Jesus and is healed. Eiesland argues that this text represents the forgiveness of sin and physical healing as equivalent: Jesus asks, "Which is easier, to say, 'Your sins are forgiven you,' or to say, 'Stand up and walk'?" (v. 23).[7] Jesus goes on to say that he commands the man to stand up "so that you may know that the Son of Man has authority on earth to forgive sins" (v. 24). Similarly, Jesus in John 5:14 warns the invalid he has cured: "Do not sin any more, so that nothing worse happens to you."

If we are indeed created in the image of God, the *imago Dei* in Genesis 1, where does this emphasis on perfection and the connection between disease and sin leave persons with Alzheimer's disease? On the margins, fearful in their isolation,

Denise Dombkowski Hopkins

feeling cut off and unworthy of God and the community of faith, very much like Job, alone on his dung heap. Eiesland argues that theological and cultural attempts to explain the tragedy of suffering/disease/death have resulted in a Christian "disabling theology"[8] that highlights the unusual relationship with God that a diseased or disabled one has: she or he "is either divinely blessed or damned: the defiled evildoer or the spiritual superhero."[9] Primary examples of this unusual relationship are the barren foremothers of the Hebrew Bible, whose divine curse is reversed by God for the bearing of a special son in Israel's history, for example, Sarah and Isaac, Rebecca and Jacob, Hannah and Samuel. This theology roots itself in the larger context of act/consequence or divine retribution in the Bible, that is, you get what you deserve, which I shall explore more fully later in this chapter. For now, suffice it to say that guilt, shame, resentment, and frustration are the inevitable results of this approach for people with Alzheimer's disease and their caregivers.

Explaining suffering in this way shifts the focus entirely to the patient who, in the case of Alzheimer's, is expected to battle valiantly without complaint in order to conquer the progressive deterioration of the brain. After all, "God's power is made perfect in weakness" (2 Cor. 12:9). This kind of pressure was so great for Robert Davis that at one point he observed: "The easiest thing in the world would be for me to move away into another area of the country, or run away to another church where no one knew me or had any expectations of me."[10]

Some biblical texts, especially the healing stories in the Gospels, can fuel this kind of expectation in the person with Alzheimer's. The result can be guilt and frustration for the patient, who feels she or he is not trying hard enough, and resentment on the part of caretakers. Jesus engages in an extensive healing ministry, curing people of leprosy (Luke 17:11–19), blindness (Mark 8:22–26; 10:46–52), and paralysis (Matt. 9:2–7). In Mark 5:21–34, for example, the healing story of the woman with the issue of blood, the woman comes up behind Jesus, who is surrounded by a crowd, and touches his cloak, thinking "If I but touch his clothes, I will be made well" (v. 28). Indeed, the text asserts that "immediately her hemorrhage stopped; and she felt in her body that she was healed of her disease" (v. 29). Jesus declares that it is the woman's faith, her participation in her own healing, that has made her well; he says: "Daughter, your faith has made you well; go in peace, and be healed of your disease" (v. 34). Once my favorite passage in the Gospels because of the respect it affords the human being as partner with God in healing and wholeness, I now look at this text quite differently, through the eyes of the person with progressively worsening Alzheimer's disease who feels directly the implication that those who are not healed are not trying hard enough and that they could be healed if only they had more faith. The victim is victimized twice.

Expectations of virtuous suffering create burdens for people with Alzheimer's. In order to cope with such pressure to measure up, people with Alzheimer's try to compensate and cover for their losses. Robert Davis recounts how he made careful lists of his church duties for the day so as not to forget them, and pretended to be happy and cheerful. Yet he admits that if anyone had given him an inspirational, spiritual illustration of God's healing in an attempt to aid his valiant struggle, "I would have exploded at them with all the pent-up frustration that filled and occupied my mind. How hypocritical I felt!"[11]

Unrealistic expectations generated shame for Cary Henderson, a former history professor who was diagnosed with Alzheimer's disease at age fifty-five. In the journal he kept until the disease progressed too far, he wrote that Alzheimer's "is a very come and go disease. When I make a real blunder, I tend to get defensive about it. A sense of shame for not knowing what I should have known and for not being able to think things and see things that I saw several years ago when I was a normal person."[12]

Henderson is aware, too, of the toll his disease takes on his wife. He writes: "People like your wife or husband sacrifice an awful lot and, I guess from their standpoint it is very difficult for them to see us, and vice versa. . . . We . . . misinterpret an

awful lot of things and I guess we get to be a darn nuisance. . . .
I think our caregivers, bless their souls and hearts, they do go
through a little bit of hell themselves—a lot of it—and a lot of
it because of us."[13] Henderson's and his wife's struggle with
the disease is real, not heroic. So, too, is Nancy Mair's struggle
with MS, with which she was diagnosed at age twenty-nine.
She refuses to be described as battling valiantly to meet everyone else's expectations. "I am only doing what I have to do. It's
enough."[14] As Eiesland observes about Mair's story, "suffering
. . . has few heroes, least of all those who wish to live ordinary
lives."[15]

Future, eschatological hope undergirds a theology of virtuous suffering which tends to turn its back on the present; the
suffering of one's affliction is a temporary means of purifica-
tion that must be endured heroically for heavenly rewards.
Paul's "thorn in the flesh," "a messenger from Satan," in
2 Corinthians 12:7–10 illustrates this theme; the thorn is a sign
of divine grace. The poor man Lazarus, "covered with sores" in
Luke 16:19–31, stayed hungry by the rich man's table and endured the dogs licking his sores but was rewarded by being
"carried away by the angels to be with Abraham" (v. 22) while
the rich man died and was tormented in Hades.

The entire book of Job offers a protest against the traditional
idea of virtuous suffering and a retributive God even as it carefully articulates the traditional view through the eyes of Job's
so-called friends. The narrative prologue to Job, chapters 1 and
2, posits Job's suffering, the loss of his family and wealth, and
the "loathsome sores" "from the sole of his foot to the crown of
his head" which he scraped with a potsherd, as a divine test under which Job must bear up. Job himself embraces this view in
his harsh rebuke to his wife, who wanted him to curse God and
die (2:10): "Shall we receive the good at the hand of God, and
not receive the bad?" he demands. This is the patient, heroic
Job extolled, romanticized, and imposed upon us by the Christian tradition. Its legacy is the modern proverb, "the patience
of Job," which seems to ignore the rest of the book.

The Job of the poetry section of the book, which begins in

chapter 3, is much different. This is the angry Job who refuses to accept the explanations for his suffering offered by his so-called friends. Eliphaz insists that Job has done something to deserve his present condition—he just hasn't looked hard enough to identify it: "Think now, who that was innocent ever perished? . . . As I have seen, those who plow iniquity and sow trouble reap the same" (4:7–8). We can only wonder where Eliphaz has been as he asserts that the world makes sense and affirms God's just system of rewards and punishments. Hasn't he read the newspapers, watched TV, seen the innocent suffering all around him? Eliphaz even argues that suffering is good for Job. It is disciplinary: "How happy is the one whom God reproves; therefore do not despise the discipline of the Almighty. . . . For God strikes, but God's hands heal" (5:17–18). Easy for Eliphaz to say—he is not the one on the dung heap scraping his sores.

Job's response says as much in 6:28: "But now, be pleased to look at me; for I will not lie to your face." Womanist theologian Emilie Townes offers a similar protest in her poem:

> evil is a force outside us
> suffering makes you stronger
> lies
> lies
> lies
> to my very deepest soul
> there is a troubling in my soul[16]

Eliphaz would have us see Job's suffering as a gift from God to make him stronger or more faithful. As my dear friends Alan Johnson and Martie McMane, former secretaries for church growth and evangelism in the United Church of Christ, put it after Alan's stroke: "Disease is not a gift from God, but there are gifts to be found in it."

Bildad offers corollaries to these arguments in Job 8:20–21: "See, God will not reject a blameless person, nor take the hand of evildoers. God will yet fill your mouth with laughter." In two rhetorical questions, Bildad asserts that God is a God of justice (8:3). Bildad posits suffering as a mark of God's love and urges Job to be patient. We can only wonder if God loves some of us too much and expects from us the impossible. For Bildad, suffering is temporary, and can lead to repentance: "If you seek God and make supplication to the Almighty, if you are pure and upright, surely then God will rouse the divine self for you" (8:5–7). Zophar offers the harshest pastoral "care" of all to Job: "Know then that God exacts of you less than your guilt deserves" (11:6b). With friends like this, who needs enemies? Just as in Nathan's parable of the ewe lamb in 2 Samuel 12, which tricks King David into pronouncing judgment against himself for his sin with Bathsheba—"*you* are the man!"—we, like Job's friends, forget too quickly our own experiences on the dung heap and fail to honor the pain of others.

How heartbreaking that some folks actually do approach the suffering of people with Alzheimer's as Job's friends did, as Rev. Robert Davis attests. He writes of his unrealistic fears and guilt that he had done something against God, reinforced by well-meaning people: "Like Job's comforters, misdirected friends unwittingly compound the afflicted person's perceived spiritual problem."[17] In their defense, however, these well-meaning folk take their cues from the church, which reinforces the concept of heroic suffering.

In my mind, perhaps the strongest signal from the church in this regard is its emphasis on one set of Jesus' last words from the cross to the exclusion of others. Luke 23:46 is usually lifted up for study in Lent: "Father, into your hands I commend my spirit," or John 19:30: "It is finished." Ignored because they make us uncomfortable are Jesus' anguished words in Matthew 27:45–46 and Mark 15:34, the first verse of Psalm 22: "My God, my God, why have you forsaken me?" The Suffering Servant texts in Deutero-Isaiah reinforce this emphasis upon the stoically suffering Jesus and the virtuous suffering model for those with disease and disabilities. For example, Isaiah 53:7: "He was oppressed, and he was afflicted, yet he did not open his mouth; like a lamb that is led to the slaughter, and like a sheep that before its shearers is silent, so he did not open his mouth."

These Servant texts showcase Israel's attempt to deal with the suffering of Babylonian exile in the sixth century B.C.E. They assign a positive value to the pain of exile and urge Israel to become a model from which the nations may learn. This context is ignored and silent suffering is made into an absolute as Israel's only response to exile when people with Alzheimer's and their caregivers are expected to suffer silently, imitating Jesus, whom the church saw as the ultimate Suffering Servant. This is a pastoral miscue. Womanist theologian Jacquelyn Grant warns us about the "sin of servanthood." "In fact," she writes, "African-American women have been the 'servants of servants.'" For "servanthood has been, in effect, servitude."[18]

When we lump the experience of Alzheimer's disease into a general discussion of aging, we run the risk of reinforcing the arguments of Job's friends and the image of the sufferer as heroic, stoic servant awaiting miraculous blessing as the only model in the Bible for dealing with Alzheimer's. Stephen Sapp has rightly criticized those who have overemphasized aging as fulfillment and a golden age of maturation. Experience of disease and poverty and the physical and emotional losses of aging show that aging is "not so golden." Sapp warns that "untempered optimism" can produce guilt for those who don't face each new day with joy.[19]

The need for Sapp's caution became clear to me in a recent article in the *Journal of Religion and Aging* on John Wesley's view of the aging process as reflected in his birthday journals, which he kept between the ages of fifty-one and eighty-eight. The author makes much of Wesley's "continuing note of optimism," his debunking of the glorification of youth, and his insistence that he was better off in his older years than he was in his twenties. "It seems this optimistic spirit may have been an important part in his longevity," the author speculates.[20] The implication is that those who do not share this optimism are responsible for a shortened life and the problems in aging which they experience. What a terrible burden to place on those struggling with

Alzheimer's, which has been described by a spouse of an Alzheimer's disease patient as "a funeral that never ends."[21] Indeed, Alzheimer's disease cannot clinically be viewed as part of the natural process of aging. Recent research has shown that neuritic plaques and neurofibrillary tangles are more numerous in Alzheimer's patients than in nondemented persons of the same age. This research makes it clear that Alzheimer's is "due to underlying brain pathology and not normal aging or negativism."[22] Alzheimer's "is not accelerated aging, as some researchers argue, but a unique pathological process."[23] This allows us to place Alzheimer's disease in the raw edges of human experience where it is not subject to unrealistic, optimistic expectations of graceful aging.

The ravages of the disease force us to reconsider, too, the concept of heroic suffering, especially for the caregiver. As psychologist Judah Ronch argues, long-term, progressive illness like Alzheimer's prevents the patient and caregiver from coming to terms with dying as a process within the life cycle. There is no chance for consolation or saying goodbye in this process. Survivors must "grieve the separation from and the loss of all that was the person while the person is still physically present to trigger memories of what is lost."[24] Roles change as the spouse moves from being lover to caregiver, "spouseless but married."

Alzheimer's spouse Betty Davis describes this process: "Death would be better than this—to hold on to the box when the present is used up—hoping the box can bring again the joy of the reality of the gift—but the box is empty! This is what one has to look forward to with Alzheimer's disease. The body of the one you love—devoid of all expression, of recognition, of joy—here but not here. You are destined to live only with the memory of who he was."[25] Because the losses of Alzheimer's "happen in a relentless series," new losses interrupt grief over a previous loss and a new process of grieving begins. Judah Ronch quotes spouse caregiver Myrna Doernberg: "I feel like I'm in limbo. . . . I know it is over, and yet he is there to remind me of what is no longer."[26]

Failing Brain, Faithful God

It is crucial in the struggle with Alzheimer's disease, out of respect for the personhood of the patient and the caregiver, created in the image of God, to break free from the grip of the two options of miraculous healing or heroic suffering that the Bible seems to offer, and search for other texts that can give hope without causing guilt and frustration for those with Alzheimer's. There are texts that reveal a faithful God who comforts the one with the failing brain, texts that challenge and stand in pastoral tension with texts depicting a God who punishes with disease and demands heroic suffering.

As Robert Davis so eloquently maintains: "There is still a part of that vital person living inside that sometimes helpless-looking body, a person who deserves to be treated with dignity."[27] He protests against eighteen-year-olds who call him "sweetie" or "dearie" and treat him like a kid at summer camp. Cary Henderson reveals in his journal his awareness of what is happening to him and the pain of it: "We want things to be like they used to be. And we just hate the fact that we cannot be what we used to be. It hurts like hell."[28] These people are not forgotten by God, judged by God, or expected by God to be heroes. They are, instead, loved by God unconditionally in their hurt and struggle for dignity.

God is with Alzheimer's caregivers, too, unconditionally, as they struggle with their loss of dreams for the future and their feelings of anger, frustration, loneliness, confusion, jealousy, depression, and envy. Caregivers also suffer under the heroic and judgmental expectations about suffering in the Bible. Instead, "a good enough solution" ought to be the central task of caregiving. For, as a book on caregiving strategies recommends,

> too often, caregivers evaluate their efforts against unrealistic standards. . . . Sometimes despite the well thought-out, best efforts of caregivers, persons with Alzheimer's will still react in troubling, painful ways. And it's easy for caregivers to believe that they have done something wrong, that they are somehow inadequate, that "if only" they were better or different, the outburst would never have occurred. . . . Are you dooming

yourself to feeling constantly inadequate because you unconsciously think, "If I do everything right, he'll never have an outburst"? If so it's time to re-evaluate the yardstick by which you judge yourself.[29]

Certainly God accepts us as we are and doesn't demand this kind of heroic and virtuous perfection.

What texts bring the reassurance of a faithful, nonjudgmental God who is there with us in our pain no matter what we are feeling, whether person with Alzheimer's or caregiver? Psalm 139 is one. The psalmist proclaims: "O LORD, you have searched me and known me . . . you discern my thoughts from far away" (vv. 1–2). For those caregivers who are trapped by knowing that it is "counterproductive to vent your frustrations in the presence of the person with Alzheimer's,"[30] the freedom to express their feelings to God is confirmed by the psalmist in verse 4: "Even before a word is on my tongue, O LORD, you know it completely." This is a God who is with us wherever we are on the emotional roller-coaster ride that is Alzheimer's, in whatever margins society might push the one with Alzheimer's or the caregiver: The psalmist asks rhetorically: "Where can I go from your spirit? Or where can I flee from your presence? If I ascend to heaven, you are there; if I make my bed in Sheol, you are there" (vv. 7–8).

This psalm illustrates what Robert Davis meant about his need for reversing his thinking as he struggled with his "spiritual anguish" and confusion in his fear and doubt and aloneness: "Instead of holding on to God and pulling myself up by my exuberant faith, I have to relax and have the simplest childlike faith and let Jesus hold me."[31] This theme of God with us is reiterated in the New Testament in Romans 8:38–39: "For I am convinced that neither death, nor life, nor angels, nor rulers, nor things present, nor things to come, nor powers, nor height, nor depth, nor anything else in all creation, will be able to separate us from the love of God in Christ Jesus our Lord."

The Bible speaks often of a God who has ears to hear and eyes to see everything in the life of human beings in the world.

Failing Brain, Faithful God

Psalm 35, for example, a prayer for deliverance from enemies, pleads: "You have seen, O LORD; do not be silent!" (v. 22). Even more prominent is the metaphor of God with ears to hear the cry of those in pain. The psalms are full of petitions to God to "hear" the psalmist's prayer, as for example in Psalm 5:1–2: "Give ear to my words, O LORD; give heed to my sighing. Listen to the sound of my cry." "God as hearer" counters prevailing views of God as punisher.[32]

God as hearer is the God of the exodus whose eye is especially focused upon and whose ear is especially attuned to the oppressed and suffering. God declares to Moses at the burning bush in Exodus 3:7–8: "I have *observed* the misery of my people who are in Egypt: I have *heard* their cry on account of their taskmasters. Indeed, I *know* [experience] their sufferings, and I have *come down* to deliver them from the Egyptians, and to *bring* them up out of that land to a good and broad land." Listen to the active verbs in this passage: observe, hear, know, come down, bring up. This is a God who suffers with God's people, who is intimately involved. Psalm 121 lifts up this intimacy: "[The One] who keeps Israel will neither slumber nor sleep. *Adonai* [The LORD] is your keeper. . . . The LORD will keep your going out and your coming in . . . forevermore" (vv. 4, 5, 8).

As Terence Fretheim argues: "God sees the suffering from the inside; God does not look at it from the outside, as through a window. God is internally related to the suffering of the people. God enters fully into the hurtful situation and makes it [God's] own."[33] Thus, in Isaiah 56:3–5, God declares: "Do not let the foreigner [a better translation is 'newcomer'] joined to [the LORD] say, 'The LORD will surely separate me from his people'; and do not let the eunuch say, 'I am just a dry tree.' For thus says the LORD: . . . I will give them an everlasting name that shall not be cut off." Abraham Joshua Heschel spoke in the same way of the divine pathos evidenced in the prophetic texts, such as Jeremiah 2:31–32, in which God feels pained and offended by Israel's sinful behavior and expresses that pain in a series of rhetorical questions. "Raise a wailing over *us*" reveals God's own weeping in Jeremiah 9:17–18.[34] God's involvement with the people's misery also occurs with individuals, as can be seen in psalms such as Psalm 23: "Even though I walk through the valley of the shadow of death, I fear no evil; for you are with me" (v. 4) and Psalm 16:8: "I keep the LORD always before me; because God is at my right hand, I shall not be moved." This is no KINGAFAP God, as Brian Wren has said; this is not "the King-God-Almighty-Father-Protector" ruling in absolute power alone in the heavens.[35]

Fretheim decisively relates "the desire of God for accessibility and closeness" to promise. As Haggai 2:4–5 puts it: "I am with you, says the LORD of hosts, according to the promise that I made you."[36] Fretheim also cites Jacob's dream at Bethel, in which God promises Jacob, "I am with you and will keep you wherever you go" (Gen. 28:15). Through Moses, God promises the Israelites in Exodus 20:24: "In every place where I cause my name to be remembered I will come to you and bless you," and again in Exodus 29:45: "I will dwell among the Israelites, and I will be their God." God limits God's freedom by these promises; "God will do what God says God will do; God will be faithful to God's own promises."[37] God's remembering is the essence of God's covenant loyalty, of God's *hesed*, often poorly translated as "steadfast love" or "loving-kindness." God promises to take God's relationship with us seriously. God will be with persons with Alzheimer's disease and with caregivers in their suffering.

Robert Davis recognizes this when he writes: "Many Christians have found that when life completely tumbles in, when they are without strength or any hope or help for themselves, or when their minds become too tangled to even hold thoughts, that God overrides the circumstances and . . . comes to minister to them at the very point of their need."[38] Herein lies the hope for people struggling with Alzheimer's.

Finally, there is this text from Deutero-Isaiah, 49:14–18, in which God reassures a suffering Zion who fears "the LORD has forsaken me, my LORD has forgotten me." Robert Davis writes of the many "terror-filled" times in his journey into Alzheimer's disease in which "I feel so cut off and alone from my dear friend Jesus."[39] He tells of how at those times he would cry out to God:

Failing Brain, Faithful God

"Remember me, I am still your servant. . . . How can you leave me at a time like this?"[40] So, too, Zion, symbolizing the people Israel, feels cut off from God, forsaken and forgotten. But God reassures Zion: "Can a woman forget her nursing child, or show no compassion for the child of her womb? Even these may forget, yet I will not forget you. See, I have inscribed you on the palms of my hands." As one child described it during a children's sermon at my church, Zion is God's tattoo, always visible. God will remember, even as the person with Alzheimer's disease slowly forgets.

3
Memory:
The Community Looks Backward

STEPHEN SAPP

*W*inston Churchill was once invited to address the national convention of the Women's Christian Temperance Union in London (an unusual invitation indeed, many would say). The president introduced him graciously enough, citing his many achievements and awards, but she concluded, "In all candor, ladies, I must point out that to his shame, Sir Winston is reported to have imbibed enough spirits to fill this great hall to the level of your heads." Churchill stepped up to the podium amid a disapproving murmur, looked out over the heads of the audience, raised his eyes to the high ceiling of the great ballroom, shook his head sadly, and said ruefully, "So much to do, and so little time." One cannot help but feel a little bit that way when addressing the topic of theological dimensions of Alzheimer's disease—so much to do, and so little time!

At the outset, a brief response needs to be made to a basic question that might be anticipated in this context, namely, why bother presenting a *theological* perspective on Alzheimer's disease at all? After all, who really cares about theology in this scientific, materialistic age? It may make sense in a book of this nature to include biblical perspectives because many people still turn to scripture for guidance and comfort in times of need, and a pastoral care point of view promises practical, concrete suggestions for those struggling to cope with this difficult illness. But *theology*, that abstract, usually incomprehensible speculation engaged in by professors sitting in their ivory towers—who needs it?

In addition to asserting that theology does not have to fit that dreary description, many people would want to affirm quite strongly that theology does matter! How one deals with life depends ultimately on how one understands God, and that is what theology is. Theology—one's understanding of God—makes a difference in the ways human beings live with one another, in the ways they deal with the pain and suffering of this life, in the joy that comes from service to those in need, and in the ways they approach their own death and the deaths of others. Theology becomes especially important in addressing issues like coping with Alzheimer's disease, which raises fundamental questions about the nature and meaning of human life itself, the concept of individual identity and personhood, obligations to one another, and so forth.

Indeed, one's basic view of aging, and thus of people who are elderly (and perhaps especially cognitively impaired), is not a scientific, factual matter at all, though obviously certain facts are relevant. The question of attitudes toward aging—what it *means* to grow old and how one should relate to people who are old—is a theological/philosophical question, that is, a question of value and ultimately of faith. Modern scientific medicine can describe better and better the biological processes that bring about the aging of the human organism, and the social sciences can study the impact that growing older has on individuals and various groups of individuals. What science simply cannot offer, however—on its own terms—is *meaning*. Modern science can provide the *means* to live longer and healthier lives, but it is utterly powerless to offer any *meaning* to live for. As C. J. Dippel so aptly put it, natural science "teaches us a method, but it does not teach us what we ought to do," an assessment echoed somewhat more poetically by

Stephen Sapp

G. de Santillana when he said, "The God of physics is there to give us what we wish, but not to tell us what we ought to wish for."[1]

Too often in contemporary postmodern society, however, purely pragmatic considerations or assessments that are thought to be clearly "factual" are the basis for action, with little thought given to the underlying values that should—and actually do—inform all decisions, whether mundane or momentous. When people who purport to be "faithful" take this approach in regard to the kinds of issues being considered in this book, we might be tempted to paraphrase Jesus (who admittedly was addressing a different matter): "What more are you doing than others? Do not even the [nonbelievers] do the same?" (Matt. 5:47).

Obviously, the ways in which people deal with the issues raised by Alzheimer's disease will be greatly influenced not only by theological beliefs but also by the nature of this particular illness, an illness that the late medical essayist Lewis Thomas in 1981 labeled the "disease of the century." Certainly one should not downplay the horrors associated with *any* illness, especially chronic, degenerative illnesses that occur increasingly as life spans are extended and a population ages. But Alzheimer's and other dementias are particularly pernicious. Many illnesses deprive a person only of the *present:* One becomes ill, feels more or less miserable depending upon the nature and severity of the illness, seeks treatment, and recovers after a relatively brief period of time, suffering the loss only of that time when he or she was actually ill. Other illnesses, for which no cure exists, take away not only a person's present but also the *future* by prematurely ending the individual's life. Alzheimer's disease, however, robs the sufferer not only of the present and the future but also of the *past* as all memory of prior events, relationships, and persons slips away.

Clearly then, the concepts of time, memory, and history are central in any theological consideration of this illness and its impact on those it touches. In contrast to the Eastern religions, which affirm the existence of an eternal world distinct from and

Memory: The Community Looks Backward

even in opposition to the world of time, the Western religious tradition is based on the belief that the eternal has actively intervened in time. These interventions constitute a sacred history, the history of the *mirabilia Dei,* the "marvelous deeds of God," which in fact lie at the heart of the faith that Christians affirm. In these deeds God has come to human beings in self-revelation, and it is to these deeds—as recorded in the scriptures that are so crucial to the Western religions—that believers turn to discover what the will of that God is for God's people.

Thus the prospect of losing memory, of no longer being able to recall this sacred history, creates a significant problem for such a belief system. Oliver Sacks, in his classic *The Man Who Mistook His Wife for a Hat,* opens chapter 2 with a quotation from the "recently translated memoirs" of Luis Buñuel. Although he is speaking in a purely personal vein, Buñuel could just as well be reflecting the classical view of the Western religious tradition:

> You have to begin to lose your memory, if only in bits and pieces, to realize that memory is what makes our lives. Life without memory is no life at all. . . . Our memory is our coherence, our reason, our feeling, even our action. Without it, we are nothing.[2]

Is this the way it is? Are human beings really nothing without memory? Or is there perhaps something more? Sacks later quotes a personal letter from A. R. Luria, a researcher and practitioner famous for his work with amnesia patients. With regard to those in whom little or no hope exists for any recovery of their memory, Luria asserts,

> But [human beings] do not consist of memory alone. [They have] feeling, will, sensibilities, moral being—matters of which neuropsychology cannot speak. And it is here, beyond the realm of impersonal psychology, that you may find ways to touch [them], and change [them]. . . . Neuropsychologically, there is little or nothing you can do; but in the realm of the Individual, there may be much you can do.[3]

Stephen Sapp

If modern scientific medicine cannot speak on this matter, the question necessarily arises: What resources exist in the Western religious tradition that might assist on this journey, that might offer some guidance through what many persons with Alzheimer's disease and their caregivers experience as, if not a dark night of the *soul,* certainly a dark night of the *mind?*

Several years ago I was invited to give the keynote address at the ninth annual Symposium on Ministry with the Aging at Kanuga Conference Center near Hendersonville, North Carolina. The theme of the symposium—and thus the title of my keynote—was "Aging Together: Building the City of God." Given the last three words of the title, it was natural to seek inspiration in the thought of that great Christian theologian Augustine of Hippo, and especially in his classic work by that same name, *City of God.* Unfortunately, nothing in the book helped at all with that talk! One thing I did run across in *City of God,* however, reminded me of an intriguing essay in the *Hastings Center Report* by Gilbert Meilaender.[4] Many of his points are relevant to the theme of this book and the issues I address in this chapter and in chapter 6. A reference Augustine makes in Book 20, chapter 20, in his discussion of the vexing question of what resurrected human bodies will be like, offers some especially fertile soil to till concerning the topic under consideration here.

In that passage, Augustine refers to human beings as *terra animata,* that is, "animated earth." This reference may surprise those who cannot see Augustine as anything other than the source par excellence within the Christian tradition of a Manichaean, Neoplatonic dualism that denigrates the importance of the physical body in favor of the soul. Augustine's language, however, should not come as a surprise to anyone who knows the Adam and Eve story, the second account of creation in Genesis 2, with which Augustine was clearly very familiar because it serves as the basis for his interpretation of human sexuality (though, of course, what he did with the story in that regard is lamentable). In fact, Augustine's discussion of this critical section of the Bible is the context in which he uses the phrase just cited:

"To earth you will go" [Gen.3:19] means, we may be sure, "On losing your life you will go back to what you were before you received life," that is, "when the breath of life has left you will be what you were before you received that breath" (for, as we know, it was into a face of earth that God "breathed the breath of life" when "man was made a living soul"). It is tantamount to saying, "You are *animated earth,* which you were not before: you will be inanimate earth, as you were before."[5]

What does it mean to contemporary Christians that according to this story, when Yahweh (God) created the human race the procedure of choice was the forcing of God's breath into a body fashioned from the earth? Technical interpretive questions abound concerning the precise meaning of this passage, questions that go well beyond the scope of this chapter. Still, several points of value to this discussion can be made without getting too deeply into controversy.

Most fundamentally, it appears indisputable that the "breath of life" (Heb. *nishmathayyim*) that God breathes into the man *(ha-'adam)* cannot be equated with the mind, the cognitive faculties, rationality, self-awareness, or anything of the kind. Rather, it appears to be exactly what the Hebrew says it is, the "force of life," vitality, the animating principle that turns what previously was simply *terra* a lump of clay, into *terra animata,* living, breathing, animated flesh, described as *nephesh hayyah* in Genesis 2:7 (a contemporary analogy might be a robot and the electricity that "animates" or "vitalizes" it, changing what was merely *machina,* a collection of metal, plastic, and wires, into *machina animata,* a moving, active entity).

Thus only after the inspiration of this life force does the creature that God has fashioned from the earth become a "living being," a description, not incidentally, that is shared with the "creeping things" of Genesis 1:20 and the animals and birds of Genesis 2:19 and 9:15–16 that God creates in much the same fashion. It is clear from this common terminology that it is not

Stephen Sapp

human reason or cognitive capacity that constitutes the endowment from God that gives humans life and makes them more than mere bits of dirt.

Second, the later course of this idea in the Hebrew scriptures suggests that the living being that humans become through God's gift of the life force ceases to exist only when that person dies in the conventional understanding of the word, not when the person loses self-consciousness or the ability to make rational decisions. For example, in Genesis 35:18, Rachel's death is described this way: "As her life-force was departing (for she died) . . . " (author's translation). Thus it seems that whatever God gives to humans that makes them *living* beings continues with them until they actually die, not merely until they lose their cognitive faculties.

This story of human creation as *terra animata* reflects and probably underlies the biblical view of human nature itself, a view that is quite helpful in trying to deal constructively with the issues that Alzheimer's disease raises. Although the Hebrew scriptures use such terms as "flesh" and "spirit" ("body" and "soul"), they do not depict these as separate substances that only coincidentally or unfortunately cohere. This is the view most people today tend to assume when they hear such terms, and it is based on the Greek ideas that have infiltrated contemporary Western culture. Rather, in the biblical view these two terms describe *inter*dependent elements that together make up the human being, *both* of which are necessary for human existence. The late Paul Ramsey, one of this century's preeminent Protestant ethicists, put it well when he wrote that the human being "is an embodied person in such a way that he *is* in important respects his body. He is the body of his soul no less than he is the soul (mind, will) of his body."[6] Instead of considering the soul (or will or personality) to be the "real" person, and the body to be something almost incidental that the person "has," it is more accurate according to the biblical understanding to say that human beings *are* bodies, that they are both animated, "ensouled" bodies and incarnate, "enfleshed" souls.

Thus the mental and physical activities of the individual are merely different manifestations of the same underlying "living being." The person does not *have* a body that is somehow fundamentally different from and even alien to the soul that exists within it, as if "person" were more elemental, a distinct existent that is a possessor of the body. Rather the person *is* a body that is alive, animated by the life force that comes from God. In short, the "person" does not exist apart from the body, which is the outward manifestation of the total reality that includes it (to get a feel for the point being made here, ask yourself, "Exactly what is it that I really mean when I use the word 'I'?").

Clearly, then, in the original Hebrew understanding the body cannot be seen as a prison from which the soul struggles to escape: A person simply perishes if body and "soul" are separated because what is usually thought of today as the soul is really just the principle of life itself—that which makes the body alive. So inextricably are they united that when the life force departs, the body dies and nothing is left as a separate entity to pass on to another existence.

Christians of course believe that something does go on living after this life is over, but it is important to note exactly what it is that Christians affirm in this regard—not at all the "immortality of the *soul*" (a rather Greek notion, actually) but precisely the "resurrection of the *body*" (a very Hebraic concept, as just described)! Why is this significant? If body and soul *are* inextricably linked to make up the human person, then the only eternal life possible *must be* as a body because there simply is no such thing as an independent soul that can exist disembodied. Embodiedness is essential to who humans beings are because it is only *as bodies* that they exist. Attempting to describe in this life exactly what that resurrection body will be like can be nothing but idle speculation—no one can possibly know— but Christians do affirm that eternal existence with God will be in some kind of bodily form, not as ethereal spirits (see 1 Corinthians 15 for Paul's struggle with this issue).

What happened to this rather simple, straightforward biblical understanding of human nature? Many things over the course of millennia—including quite a few Greeks, especially

Stephen Sapp

perhaps Gnostics and Manichaeans, and widespread ascetic philosophies, both within and outside the church. But credit (or blame) for the final dismantling probably belongs to the French mathematician René Descartes. Dualistic epistemologies and anthropologies existed long before Descartes proposed his in the first half of the seventeenth century. For a number of reasons, though, he struck a particularly responsive chord in a time that needed philosophical underpinnings for the reductionistic approach to the world that characterized the rising scientific method.

In barest outline, Descartes proposed that all reality is divided into two realms: *res extensa,* the world of bodies characterized by extension and rigid adherence to precise mathematical laws; and *res cogitans,* the world of unextended, thinking, spiritual substance that is independent of the first realm. Because living bodies are extended, they must be part of the *res extensa.* Animals are in fact machines or automata, totally determined by physical laws, and the same judgment applies to human bodies, at least insofar as those bodies function largely automatically and without conscious attention.[7]

Descartes arrived at his dualistic view of reality via the method of universal doubt, in which the only thing unable to be doubted is the doubting *self* (hence his famous dictum, *Cogito, ergo sum*—"I think, therefore I am"—significantly, an identification of disembodied *thought* with "real" existence). Obviously, this approach led to a dualistic view of human beings: The individual is composed of two substances, an extended machine for a body and an independent, unextended mind. It takes little effort to determine which one came to be seen as the more important one, in fact, the *only* valuable one.

A cardinal methodological axiom of science arose from difficulties the Cartesian scheme encountered in explaining the relationship between these two separate realms of existence, namely, the concept of the "detached observer," objectively scrutinizing and recording. Because the body is but a machine (though an amazingly complex one), it is proper procedure for the scientific mind to observe it only from without, especially given that Cartesian dualism suggests an unbridgeable gap between the observing mind and the observed matter. Thus today, when minds observe a human "machine" that lacks the traits that such minds recognize as akin to themselves—rationality, cognition, self-directed will—and when those minds are predisposed to see the only valuable part of the person to be precisely that which has been lost, it is not hard in the Cartesian scheme to take the next step and deny humanity to such an entity.

What is really at issue, then, is the fundamental question of precisely what one thinks constitutes the *person,* the individual *self.* And contemporary Western thought has reached a point today of great comfort in adopting a radical dualism in its basic anthropology. The prevailing view seems to have elaborated from this dualistic stance two at best questionable assumptions, as Gilbert Meilaender suggests: first, that humans exist in some kind of timeless, disembodied form that is the "real self," an essential "I" somehow separate from the body and all the experiences that that body provides the person and that make up his or her personal history; and second, that there is one particular time in each person's life when "I am really I," a period toward which all that has gone before has pointed and after which all that follows is somehow less than the essential "I," even to the point that that "I" actually is lost.

The central problem with this contemporary understanding of personhood is that it separates the "person" from the biological nature or embodied self that is the only locus and vehicle for the personal history that constitutes living. It is interesting that an age that claims to have moved beyond metaphysics, that is almost universally characterized as materialistic and historical, has arrived at a concept of the person that is thoroughly divorced from both the material body and the history of that individual's life. Indeed, it is rather ironic that a society that prides itself on its basis in scientific method, that grounds its approach to truth in a basically reductionistic view that claims the only objective reality is the material, that has rejected the notion of timeless Truth in favor of relativity in nearly every aspect of human life one can imagine—that such a society has arrived at a point where it in effect disregards the material and historical (in this case human bodies and the events they have experienced that make up people's personal histories) in favor of some immaterial, essentialist notion of personhood. As Meilaender observes, "How wrong we would be to suppose that ours is a materialistic age, when everything we hold central to our person is separated from the animated earth that is the body."[8]

Of course, human beings are not *just* bodies, but they are assuredly and undeniably that. Indeed, it may even be argued that the body is the most important of the aspects of personhood, at least as far as earthly life is concerned. That is, if a person's *body* is destroyed (or its vitality clearly lost), no one would claim that being is still a human person in the sense in which that term is normally used, that is, to denote someone who is automatically considered to possess a special value that cannot be wantonly violated, a being worthy of protection from harm, and so forth. To use a rather graphic illustration: Few would claim that stabbing a *corpse* constitutes murder (though the case argued above is supported by the fact that *even after* the vitality of the body is lost, even after the "person" is clearly gone, the inanimate *body* still retains enough importance even in contemporary thought to generate the widespread feeling that it should be treated with due respect—witness the deep concern about recovering and identifying the bodies of victims of air crashes).

On the other hand, if that same person were to retain *bodily* integrity and vitality but to lose consciousness, rationality, the capacity to make autonomous choices for himself or herself (though some people are beginning to argue today there is no longer a human person at stake), most people would simply take the commonsense position that of course this is still a human being even if some or even most of these capacities have been lost. Serious questions, not to mention criminal charges, would be directed toward the knife wielder (this example is not intended to pre-judge what is appropriate or not with regard to certain medical decisions at the end of life when nothing more can be done to cure a person's illness).

Indeed, if memory is so important, one has to ask where those memories came from in the first place? And the answer is unarguable: They came from experiences that the person has had in and through his or her body. The body is the only avenue human beings have for interacting with the world and other persons around them, and thus for creating memories and a personal history. Is it not curious that many people today are so quick to disregard this fact and to consider the "person" to be lost when the memories are lost, with no regard for the value of the organism that permitted those memories to be made in the first place or for the importance of that organism's ongoing personal history?

As mentioned earlier, quite instructive in this regard is a central doctrine that most Christians affirm every Sunday and that was part of Jewish belief in Jesus' day, namely, the "resurrection of the body." This idea, whatever one believes it to mean, is a ringing affirmation of the position just articulated. If the condition in which the believer is going to spend eternity with God is in some way em*bodied* (though not necessarily in a physical body as experienced in this life), it is hard to imagine a stronger statement of the importance of this aspect of human nature. If the *body* is important enough to be resurrected in some form for eternity, to be the apparently essential vehicle for that eternal relationship with the Divine that lies at the heart of the Christian promise, it logically ought to be seen as fairly significant in this life. Because of the deeply rooted dualism described earlier, however, to whatever extent moderns believe in eternal life, they seem much more comfortable with the idea of a disembodied immortal soul than a resurrected eternal body. Whether that preference makes more sense or whether it is easier to conceive and to explain how such a thing might be, it certainly cannot be seen as more in line with the teachings of the basic documents of the Christian faith. Neither, incidentally, as Reinhold Niebuhr once pointed out, is there any more empirical evidence for it than there is for some kind of bodily resurrection.[9]

Space limitations preclude detailed consideration of one other Christian doctrine that supports the position being articulated here, a doctrine that theologian Emil Brunner called the "fundamental Christian truth." This cardinal belief is of course the incarnation, the affirmation that in the human being Jesus, God is in some mysterious way directly present on earth. It seems so self-evident as to need no defense that this doctrine is the demonstration par excellence of the value of the body as an essential part of who human beings are. Though God could (and did) communicate with human beings in other ways, "when the fullness of time had come" (Gal. 4:4) God chose to assume human form—to become embodied—in order to redeem humankind. And it was quite important to the early church to make clear to all that this Jesus was "fully human," not just the "real" Spirit-God *seeming* to inhabit a body. When this view is taken together with the doctrines of creation and resurrection of the body already presented, it is reasonable to conclude that even when rational function is lost, God may still value the human *body* enough to stay in some kind of relationship to it.

Perhaps in the final analysis, then, instead of the contemporary dualistic tendency to see the *real* person as something different from embodied existence, Augustine's view of the *terra animata,* which is really just another expression of the biblical view of the human person as a psychophysical unity, is a more accurate reflection of the reality that human beings both experience in themselves and observe in others. That is, the "I" so important to contemporary American culture is really the sum total of one's experiences, the natural history of one's life, however long or short, a life that can be lived on this earth only in and through the body, in both its growth and its decline. Each human life consists of a story that began before that person was aware of it and therefore presumably can continue after he or she again ceases to be aware of it.

Yet today there is increasing pressure to excerpt only a part of that story and to assert that that segment, which has come to be seen as genuine "personhood," is the only part with value. As Meilaender points out, however, even after a person ceases to be *aware* of the part in the story that is his or her life, that story certainly continues *physically*—in the body's ongoing ingestion and utilization of nourishment, in its struggles against injury and infection, and simply in the ongoing presence of the body that has always been the location of the "I" that loved ones and friends have known.[10] It continues *interpersonally* in *their* ongoing interactions with the person, if only as his or her caregivers and even if his or her contributions to the relationship are limited or have ceased altogether. And it continues *socially* by virtue of the fact that until the *totality* that the Western religious tradition affirms is really the person ceases to be, that person does still occupy a place in the community, however limited (to put it crassly, someone's survivors cannot collect on life insurance or distribute the estate just because the person has lost his or her cognitive capacity). Thus even when one's rational capacities fade or fail completely, the "I" that consists of much more than those capacities continues to exist—diminished, to be sure, but still worthy of the dignity and respect due to all those who are created in God's own image.

Earlier Luis Buñuel was quoted as saying, "Life without memory is no life at all. . . . Without it, we are nothing." When one sees the word "memory" in connection with Alzheimer's disease, the obvious (and correct) assumption is that the *patient's* memory is at issue. After all, one of the worst aspects of this illness (many would say *the* worst) is that it robs its victims of their memory and thus raises the tough questions that have been explored in this chapter concerning personal identity and even person*hood*. So it is clearly appropriate to have concentrated up to this point on the impact of Alzheimer's disease on the individual.

It is also fitting, however, to redirect the focus (and explain the title of this chapter) by suggesting that it is not just the memory of the person with Alzheimer's that matters, at least in a Western religious context. Throughout the history of the

"Peoples of the Book," the *collective* memory of the community has been central to believers' self-understanding. Indeed, in certain periods it was probably more important than any sense of individual identity (recall, for example, the notion of "corporate personality" made famous by H. Wheeler Robinson[11]). This emphasis is evident in Western theology, ethics, and certainly ritual: In Christianity the central sacrament is precisely a collective remembrance of the life (and death) of one individual; in Judaism the key rite is a similar community recollection of the formative event for the covenant people, the Passover preceding the exodus.

Thus it seems appropriate to conclude this chapter with a brief consideration of the guidance that might come from a more *corporate* understanding of the word "memory" for dealing with those *individuals* who may be losing (or have already lost) theirs.[12] It goes without saying that contemporary American society is very individualistic, almost certainly the most radically so in human history. At the heart of the American approach to life is the deeply held belief that in the final analysis, each person is a discrete, self-sufficient monad whose greatest achievement is to "do one's own thing" according to the light of one's own reason (or often, it seems, one's emotions). This attitude is reflected, for example, in the fact that the key value for contemporary bioethics is "autonomy." Certainly one would not want to advocate the loss of individuality and autonomy—recent events in eastern Europe and elsewhere have demonstrated that human beings apparently can have these values taken from them for only so long before they must demand them back. Nonetheless, many people today think the United States has gone too far in this regard, and this excess has a significant impact upon the topic of this chapter.

Once again, a helpful corrective is to be found in the basic documents of the Christian faith, especially the Hebrew scriptures. The importance of memory in general for the biblical religions has already been mentioned. More specifically now, the idea of what may be called "corporate memory" (or the memory of the community) can provide a useful perspective on the issues under consideration. In ancient Israel, one of the reasons that the "elders" were so highly respected was precisely because they were the depositories of the memories of the covenant people. The continued existence (or at least well-being) of the people depended on remembering that Yahweh had intervened in a unique way in history on their behalf and had given them certain responsibilities to fulfill if Yahweh were to continue to bless them. Among many illustrations, a particularly clear one is given in Deuteronomy 32:7, when Moses takes the people of Israel to task for their faithlessness to the God who had been ever faithful to them: "Remember the days of old, consider the years long past; ask your father, and he will inform you; your elders, and they will tell you." Clearly Moses' emphasis here is on the importance of the memories of the elders, who had lived long and experienced much (including frequently the "sacred history" itself). It is of course exactly these kinds of memories that are progressively lost in Alzheimer's disease.

Another of the responsibilities of the elders, however, was to produce offspring and convey to them the memories of the people, which of course would then include the memory of (i.e., remembering) those elders and their role in the history of the people. In short, if people today can overcome their sense of radical individualism enough to see themselves as truly part of the community, then the community can not only remember them when they are no longer here but also can remember *for* them when they cannot do so for themselves. The Borg from *Star Trek: The Next Generation* may seem a strange illustration in this context, but the concept being described here is rather like the Borg's "organic" unity of shared thought and memory, in which *individual* experiences and thus in a sense the individuals who have those experiences become part of the *corporate* consciousness. Christians will probably be more comfortable with Paul's image of the organic unity of the body of Christ, which can be interpreted in somewhat the same way (see Romans 12 and especially 1 Corinthians 12).

Specifically, it seems that caregivers can be not only givers

Stephen Sapp

of care but bestowers of a kind of immortality by recalling for others around them what the person with Alzheimer's disease no longer can recall in order to strengthen the remembering of that person and to keep his or her role in the story of the community alive in the corporate memory. In fact, many caregivers may miss out on an important opportunity in this regard. Because short-term memory seems to fade before long-term memory in those with dementia, many tend to recall and repeat stories and experiences from their distant past. The common reaction of caregivers is to get irritated and frustrated at hearing these "old stories," especially given the repetition. Perhaps those caring for the person should instead listen carefully to and even record these stories and learn from them. After all, many of the stories concern times when the caregivers were not around, and if they are allowed to be lost with the fading memory of the person with Alzheimer's disease, then that part of the family's and the broader community's history is gone forever. In addition, caregivers need to record their own struggles, sufferings, and triumphs, because those also are important parts of the history not only of the caregiver but also of the person being cared for. If they are lost, then that person is in a sense lost even more.[13]

Of course, it is also possible to speak of *God's* memory in this light. Whether the individual remembers, or even whether the community remembers for the individual, the Western religious tradition certainly affirms that *God* remembers. Some comfort, therefore, can be found in the fact that God's memory is unfailing, even if that of any given human being is defective or even totally lost. God never forgets.

Many contemporary Americans appear to have lost their appreciation for this "community of memory" (it seems more alive in certain subcultures). If it has been lost, though, it is not because it is alien to the Christian theological tradition. Most Christians still affirm it every Sunday when they express belief in the "communion of saints"—but that discussion must wait until chapter 6, where the focus will shift from the past and memory to the future and hope.

Love, Wisdom, and Justice: Transcendent Caring

JAMES W. ELLOR

*T*he experience of one family or even one family caregiver and that of another is likely to be different. Some families can see a real blessing in their relationships with one who has Alzheimer's disease. Other families see caring for seniors with Alzheimer's disease as a nightmare. To some extent professionals can predict this relationship based on previous levels of exchange and bonding. However, research has not found all the critical variables. Whether or not caregiving is seen as a positive experience, most persons see it as a challenge for the entire family system.

Most of us when we think about our parents assume that they will be able to take charge of themselves. Indeed for adult children, it is often difficult to see parents in any other way. With the advance of the disease, the person with Alzheimer's progressively loses the ability to master the environment. As this happens, personal safety may quickly become an issue. Family members, friends, and staff of nursing homes and adult day-care centers need to step in and become interpreters of reality and functional manipulators of the environment on behalf of the senior. We are all familiar with this type of dependence—infants. But adults who have Alzheimer's disease are *not* infants. They *are* adults. Even if some of their behaviors are found in the younger population, a cognitively impaired adult needs to be treated with the respect and dignity due to a person with a history of being that spans fifty, seventy, or even ninety years.

Part of the challenge of caring for an older adult with Alzheimer's disease is in the fact that he or she is a person of history. We are that person's friend, neighbor, or family member through a history of relationship that generally started after that person was an infant. The history carried by our parents is not simply their history, it is that of their children—us—as well. Our love, friendship, and concern for the person who has Alzheimer's disease are based to some extent on that history and are threatened by the loss of memory experienced by the person. In many ways it is easier to experience the death of one that we care about, since with death, the history of this person in this life ends. For the Alzheimer patient, history seems to continue in a way that family and friends feel is contradictory to the nature of the previous relationship. To that end, *some* families find it easier to think of the parent they used to know as dead, in order to live with the remaining remnants of the person.

Watching a Loved One
Go through the Stages

It is difficult to watch a person you love and with whom you have a relationship go through anything that is painful. If a parent or spouse loses a job, if there is serious illness or depression, family members are affected by the pain that is evident. When parents or spouses have Alzheimer's disease, they have a disease that will only get worse, that takes their memory and much of their personality, and that creates caregiving difficulties for the family. Family members often say that death of a parent or spouse would be easier for the family than living with the person with Alzheimer's. For many families, it is like watching the individual die in pieces.

Love, Wisdom, and Justice: Transcendent Caring

In the beginning, the most obvious effects of Alzheimer's disease are the changes in memory. But, forgetfulness is a symptom that in many ways can be managed. The real difficulties are when the disease affects personality features such as rigidity or the willingness to compromise. Often in the early stage of Alzheimer's disease the person becomes rigid and stubborn about making routine decisions and handling interpersonal situations. This rigidity or stubbornness is often a way the person with Alzheimer's disease tries to retain control of the environment. After all, change is difficult, but repetition can stave off situations of embarrassment about forgetfulness or inability to negotiate familiar surroundings. This stubbornness often alienates those who do not understand the nature of the disease. Even more difficult for friends to understand is the fact that people with Alzheimer's disease often won't admit there is anything wrong. And often they forbid their spouse or other family members to share this information with anyone.

This "secret" phase of personality transition is alienating and threatening to friends and family members. But unfortunately, the desire for secrecy is often well-founded. When friends, clubs, and even churches find out that the person has Alzheimer's disease, they may take away all responsibility and respect.

For some people stubbornness is not a new trait; they simply become more difficult to contend with in interpersonal situations. For others, it is new. Yet because of the "secret," even if family members know the diagnosis, they cannot help others to understand. As the disease becomes more obvious in its behavioral ramifications, management of the behavioral symptoms becomes the problem for the family. When a parent or spouse forgets the name of someone important to them or is unable to recognize the person, it is awkward. When the disease progresses to overt acting-out behaviors, or incontinence, often a line is crossed, and family members begin to discuss the need for a long-term care facility. In these final stages all the resources of the family may be needed to support the person with Alzheimer's.

James W. Ellor

The Role of the
Older Adult in the Family

As family members watch a loved one go through the stages of Alzheimer's disease, they experience more than just the impairment of the person. Each person in a family represents a set of roles or customary functions that are a part of what he or she contributes to the family unit, functions such as wage earnering, driving the family car, taking out the trash. These functions are examples of the more obvious aspects of a person's daily routine that will eventually become disrupted as he or she becomes more impaired as the result of the disease. Somewhat less obvious roles are reflected in the place in the family history which is played by this person. As a parent, he or she is one of the keepers of the childhood history of the children. As a spouse, he or she is the keeper of a relationship of intimacy which is largely unknown to anyone other than the other spouse. We have been implying that this history is positive. Yet in some instances the memories may be negative. If the person has been abusive or "difficult" in relationships with family and friends, there may be unresolved anger or grief that can never be resolved by the family members or friends once the person has Alzheimer's.

Those who work with someone who has Alzheimer's disease need to be able to see a larger picture of the person than can be observed using the physical evidence of this disease. Questions about why this happens or the meaning of life for the Alzheimer's disease patient are impossible to answer from a biological or traditional scientific perspective. For the answers we must turn to theology.

Theological Considerations

Paul Tillich offers three theological principles that can assist clergy and lay caregivers in thinking about the concerns of families who care for older adults with Alzheimer's disease: *love, wisdom,* and *justice.* As persons of faith, we are called to reflect the *love* of God in our relationships with others. Theologians such as Calvin, Tillich, and others emphasize the centrality of love in our faith. The type of transcendent love that many of us have come to know within our closest relationships is difficult to experience with those who are affected by Alzheimer's disease. Part of the disease process is the loss of concern for self and others. At times caregivers believe they do see some caring from the person with Alzheimer's, but frequently it is a fleeting expression. The only way those with advanced Alzheimer's can experience love is from those of us who care about them. Since they often cannot even say "thank you," caregivers need to turn to each other and to our faith for support. Our witness to the knowledge of God's total and complete love for each one of us as we reach out to one another is critical to the emotional support of family members and other caregivers.

Tillich notes that whoever "knows the Old Testament knows that Wisdom has a position beside God, helping Him in his Creation and then coming down into the hearts of the man or woman on the street. It is often later identified with the Christ or with his spirit" in the New Testament.[1] Wisdom is the product of experience and insight. The task of the pastoral counselor is to work with the experience of the senior to facilitate insight. The experience of each family member will be different regarding his or her relationship with the person who has Alzheimer's disease. The pastoral counselor begins by listening to the family members describe that experience. For some there may be a sense of respect and horror that this disease has taken away the dignity of the older adult. For others, possibly those whose relationships with the senior have been difficult or abusive, there is a sense of unresolvable anger. For this latter group the lack of resolution can turn into vengeance when the angry family member becomes legally responsible for the person with Alzheimer's. It may also turn into neglect, a result of the deep conflict of emotions between a feeling of filial responsibility and anger that enveloped the relationship. No matter what the nature of the relationship, the pastoral counselor needs to help family members process their feelings, both good and bad.

Those who know Tillich's work will be more familiar with his use of "power" than "wisdom" as a key point in his formula for ethical decision making. It is not clear why Tillich changed the term in this address offered late in his life. However, wisdom is in many ways a form of power. In much the same way as knowledge is power, wisdom offers the person who has it power within the context of the groups in which he or she associates.

Tillich's third principle reflects *experience.* Care for families working with older adults who have Alzheimer's disease should reflect the experience of others who have gone before us, both as professionals and as caregivers. It also needs the *experience* of the person-to-person encounter that we have had with the older adult. If we try to forget the past experiences and history that we have had with that person, or that he or she has had with other persons, then we too forget the historical organization of this unique human being for whom we are caring. Tillich notes that "in the moment in which we meet a potential person and don't acknowledge his or her as such, not only in our thinking but also in our acting, we are ourselves prevented from realizing, or actualizing, ourselves as persons."[2] The techniques developed to work with Alzheimer's disease—one-to-one communication; support for the activities of daily living, and even worship—can help us continue to respond to the challenge of caring about the person with Alzheimer's.

Tillich refers to what we have called experience as the principle of justice. Justice is the heart of the human relationship. Love, wisdom, and justice become for Tillich the three ethical norms that work together to inform ethical decision making. Families of older adults may be forced to make extremely difficult decisions. Such families can turn to their congregation and clergy for help with these decisions. Decisions made on behalf of the person with Alzheimer's disease need to reflect these principles of love, wisdom, and justice.

The challenge to our understanding of ourselves as persons who are also growing older and the challenge to our relationship with the older adult comes from a disease. It is not the will of the person with Alzheimer's to forget, to become paranoid, or to forget his or her friends. It requires all our abilities to work together to support these older adults and their family and friends during the process of this disease.

Pastoral Considerations

Applying theology and pastoral counseling in the context of working with families struggling with the needs of a person who has Alzheimer's disease must begin with an understanding of all the resources of the entire family system. Too often one person takes on the caregiving task and tries to do it all. This may be possible in early stages of the disease, but it becomes more difficult in the latter stages. When possible, it is important to engage all the resources of the family—including as many family members as possible from the beginning. At first the primary responsibilities may be centered on one or two persons, but all family members need to feel they are invested in the process. As the disease progresses, relief needs to be available for the primary caregiver. This generally implies some ability to pass the responsibilities around the family.

One of the pastoral tasks at the beginning and throughout the process of working with the cognitively impaired person is to ensure that members of the family feel the burdens of caregiving are fairly distributed. This aspect of love and justice is exercised by listening to the amount of sacrifice and feelings of "burden" expressed by each family member. Those with greater investment in the relationship with the impaired individual will often come forward to offer assistance first. They will also maintain this investment longer. However, other family members need to see the caregiving tasks as important to them as well. The ability to work together as a family becomes a part of the "wisdom" of the family system.

This ensuring of each family member's investment is important when it is possible, given the family system. The pastor or lay leader should remember, however, that existing family dynamics were not created recently. Rather, family dynamics develop over time and have a history that will be reflected in discussions of family caregiving. For example, those who have always offered leadership in decision making will continue to do so, and someone who has traditionally been the family scapegoat will also continue in this role. Some work with these family dynamics may need to be done in order to facilitate the caregiving process.

Tillich's principle of *love* is important in this discussion. Caregiving should focus on the need for love of the person which is transcendent, love that enables the caregiver to see beyond the current limitations of the impaired person. Nurturing such love may involve family discussions to tell the stories of the person and everyone's relationship with the person so that they can be remembered. It can also mean keeping in mind that the goal in caregiving is the expression of love, not the cure of the illness. Alzheimer's disease cannot be cured. It can only be maintained. If cure of the disease is sought, it will only frustrate all those involved.

A second area of concern for clergy and lay leaders is the nature of the responsibility for the impaired individual. In most states, a spouse has a different financial obligation than does an adult child. The legal aspects of responsibility need to be examined with local assistance. The moral obligation, on the other hand, may be more difficult to struggle with and important for pastoral dialogue. Tillich defines "moral acts" as those acts "in which we actualize our potentiality or our essential nature, that which we ought to be, namely, to be Persons."[3] To understand this statement, we need to recognize that Tillich saw the essential nature of the person to have existed prior to the fall of Adam when humanity was in relationship with God (Genesis 1). Thus, our potentiality is reflective of the true relationship with God. This definition offers much latitude for human understanding of what it means to care for an older family member since the total parameters of our relationship with God prior to the Fall are not fully understood by anyone. Many theologians, however, have attempted to address this.

One of the most difficult times for families comes when they feel that they are being asked to "test the ethical limits" of the relationship between adult children, their parents, and their own children, the grandchildren of the older adult. A time may come when the needs of the older adult become so time-consuming for one of the adult children that their children feel neglected. It may come when the emotional burdens of care-giving seem to shut the caregiver off from the rest of her or his life. Possibly the most difficult time is when it becomes clear that the impaired adult cannot continue to live independently and must either move to a residential facility or into the home of an adult child in order to receive the care needed. For the person with Alzheimer's disease, the type of care needed is often guidance and protection rather than heavy physical care such as that needed by a person dying from cancer or some other terminal disease. However, taking a cognitively impaired person into the family home may mean that teenagers are embarrassed to bring their friends home, or that someone has to be available in the home twenty-four hours a day.

One can argue that there are many good reasons to bring the person with Alzheimer's into the home, and there are many good reasons not to do so. On one hand, bringing the parent into a home means that he or she is not in an institution. Adult children who bring their parents into their home generally want what is best for their parents. However, some adult children may be influenced by other considerations. One common motivation is a feeling that Mom or Dad cared for their children when they were younger; therefore, the child should now return the favor by caring for the parent. The adult child may be motivated by financial concerns. One spouse may be coerced by the other spouse to take in his or her parent. Possibly the most difficult reason for caregiving is a promise given by a son to a father sometime before the father dies, that the son will never put his mother into a nursing home. This seems to make the father feel better but may be extremely unrealistic later for the mother.

Clearly there are some good reasons for bringing the person with Alzheimer's into the family, if there are other persons at home who can be available to support the primary caregivers, allowing them to leave home when necessary and to take a break from caregiving. To bring an adult who has Alzheimer's disease into the home also requires a strength in the family system that is not always available in modern society. The bond between spouses and with the extended family must be strong enough to overcome the difficulties that will arise in caregiving situations.

Our society is set up to allow caregiving for children. We have diaper changing tables in restrooms and other aids to support parents taking care of children. But when an older husband is taking care of a wife with Alzheimer's disease, there are few considerations for such basic needs as toileting in public institutions. A second problem is that the family life cycle is often reflective of adult children who have moved past serving the total dependency needs of their own children. Their lifestyles have now become such that it is extremely difficult to return to a way of living where someone needs them all the time.

A second set of considerations is possibly more reflective of spouse caregivers than adult children, though it may apply to them as well. Often spouses become caregivers for their cognitively impaired spouses. In such cases, it seems to be part of the marriage vow to love and to cherish, *in sickness and in health.* The critical concern in this context may be the quality of life for the spouse who does not have Alzheimer's disease. Often the world of the caregiving spouse shrinks to the geography of the house and maybe the grocery store. Friends often stay away, and the caregiver is alone twenty-four hours a day with a spouse who in the advanced stages of the disease often no longer knows the caregiver. The quality of life for this person becomes marginal at best.

Handling situations that test the "ethical limits" of human relationships can be extremely difficult for families. How do you know when "enough is enough"? What ethical guidelines can be used to understand when caregiving is appropriate, and when it is not? When we find ourselves unable to balance the needs of older parents with those of spouses and children, how do we make our decisions? For this discussion, three possible models may be helpful. The first is a more traditional model from John Calvin; the second, the Talmudic concept of filial responsibility; the third, from Gibson Winter. All offer a biblical basis for their arguments, but each is reflective of its culture and its time.

Three Models for Ethical Guidelines

Calvin

John Calvin never wrote a specific paper or sermon on the ethical considerations of caregiving for older adults. However, his reflections on the Fifth Commandment offer some insight into this issue. In the Fifth Commandment, "Honor your father and your mother, so that your days may be long in the land that the LORD your God is giving you" (Ex. 20:12), Calvin sees the primary focus on the word "honor." He starts this discussion by reminding the reader that charity as reflected in Colossians 3:14 reflects a need for mutual obligation between people. However, "human society cannot be maintained in its integrity, unless children modestly submit themselves to their parents, and unless those who are set over others by God's ordinance, are even reverently honored."[4] Calvin goes on to suggest that based on reason and, he implies, scripture as well, there are "three heads" to this concept of honor. The first refers to the reverence given to "the father." Calvin says, "Since, therefore, the name of Father is a sacred one, and is transferred to men by the peculiar goodness of God, the dishonoring of parents redounds to the dishonor of God Himself."[5] The second "head" is obedience. Calvin suggests that "Paul is a faithful interpreter of this commandment, where he bids 'children obey their parents'" (Eph. 6:1; Col. 3:20). Calvin writes:

> Honor, therefore, comprises subjection; so that he who shakes off the yoke of his father, and does not allow himself to be governed by his authority, is justly said to despise his father; and it will

more clearly appear from other passages, that those who are not obedient to their parents are deemed to despise them. Still, the power of a father is limited as that God, on whom all relationships depend, should have the rule over fathers as well as children.[6]

Thus, for Calvin, there are times when the father is not obedient to God and therefore, if "a father enjoins anything unrighteous, obedience is freely to be denied him."[7] However, with submission to the will of God and some moderation of wills, children should always be obedient to their parents. The final "head" for Calvin is that

> children should take care of their parents, and be ready and diligent in all their duties towards them. This kind of piety the Greeks call *antipelargia,* because storks supply food to their parents when they are feeble and worn out with old age, and are thus our instructors in gratitude. Hence the barbarity of those is all the more base and detestable, who either grudge or neglect to relieve the poverty of their parents, and to aid their necessities.[8]

Calvin seems to take the position that since parents take care of us, we then should care for them. He places this in the perspective that parents also have some obligation. First, parents should not ask for anything that is "unrighteous." For Calvin this is generally something that is inconsistent with the will or work of God. Second, parents should do all that they can to "attract" children to comply with their wishes and needs. Thus, parents who are either unrighteous, or not attempting to do their part to make the relationship with their adult children work, are not doing their part in this relationship. In these cases Calvin would seem to suggest that the adult child is justified in not honoring them.

These types of circumstances are difficult to translate into the situation common to those who have Alzheimer's disease. They are generally not able to "do their part" in these relationships. The nature of this disease slowly strips the person of any ability to control important elements of personality that generally offer the person the ability to be amiable.

Filial Responsibility

Norman Linzer in his summary of the Talmudic understanding of filial obligation[9] suggests that the primary concern
is that the child is to *honor and revere.* He notes that the Talmud
defines "honor" as requiring positive acts of service. The Talmud defines "reverence" as refraining from behavior that
might cause embarrassment, such as sitting in the father's place,
contradicting him, and speaking before one's turn. Both honor
and reverence are expressions of personal value and reflect
emotional bonds with one's parent. This is important as they are
not seen as simply "obligations" but rather as reflecting the nature of the relationship between parents and children.

The Talmud suggests that the moral obligation or duty of the
child is to support one's parents. This responsibility is a mirror
image of the parents' responsibility to support their child. The
Talmud emphasizes that one should honor a parent, not so
much for bringing the child into the world, but for the instruc-
tion the parent has given the child. The emphasis is on the relationship of the parent and child. Acts of caregiving are
important, but as expressions of *honor and reverence.*

Focusing on the
Marital Relationship

A third perspective is offered by Gibson Winter,[10] who focuses on the role of aging in society and thus the role of the
older adult in the family. Winter argues that "our family life,
concentrating as it does on the intimacy of parents with dependent children, has frozen out the grandparents."[11] Winter
understands society in the United States as fostering the attitude that most adult children should take a position of neu-
trality between the parents of the two spouses. The adult
children try to avoid slighting either set of parents by being fair
to all. He points out that this "neutral-but-equal doctrine" becomes problematic when the couple considers taking one parent into their own home.

Winter's perspective is that of the middle-aged couple. He

starts in his ethical consideration from the view that in the marriage vow

> husband and wife pledge a loyalty to one another in marriage which demands that they forsake father and mother and cleave to one another. . . . In our society, however, the covenant of intimacy is a very personal alliance. The stability of this relationship depends on the exclusion of others from equal intimacy.[12]

Winter is not trying to exclude parents from the family relationship, he is simply focusing on the needs of the middle-aged children as the center for ethical discussion.

Winter goes on to say, "The stability of personal life for parents and children rests on the fulfillment of this covenant. Neither husband nor wife has any right to set responsibility to his or her parent before this covenant of marriage. The intimacy of husband and wife with their dependent children is the prior obligation for the members."[13] It is important to note that it is this bond of intimacy which is blessed by God and is the basis of Winter's criteria for decision making. It is not the marriage relationship by itself. While Winter does not say so directly, he implies that if the intimate bond between husband and wife is not threatened or even could be enhanced by caregiving for an older adult, then this would be an appropriate criterion for taking a parent into one's home.

Winter's basis for ethical decision making is different in many ways from that of Calvin and Linzer. Where Calvin and Linzer base their process on the relationship of the parent and child, Winter offers the marriage as the platform for this decision-making process. Where Calvin and Linzer base their process on honoring the parent, Winter bases his work in the intimacy of the marital relationship. It would be hard to make a universal statement for every family as to which approach to this decision makes more sense. Clearly, some families start from a stronger conviction or bias for one approach or the other. It should also be said that each of these concepts has been taken out of a larger context for each author. For a practitioner to take either position, he or she should work from the larger context of the authors' work.

Tillich and Ethical Decision Making

Tillich in his reflections on *love, wisdom,* and *justice* sees ethical decision making as happening at the junction of a reflection on all three ideas. In some ways, these three concepts become like a filter for considering each situation. Families struggling with the needs of a person who has Alzheimer's disease can use this formula by asking three questions of each situation, "Where is love in this decision?" "What does the wisdom of the professionals involved, as well as of family and friends, seem to say?" and "Is this a just decision?" By addressing these three questions, the family finds answers to the questions in their particular situation.

Caregiving and Receiving

Studies of caregiving reported in gerontological literature, have consistently found differences in the ways men and women care for their parents. Within the marital relationship, caregiving in the sense of caring for the personal needs of the parent (personal hygiene, etc.) is almost always done by daughters and daughters-in-law. In this sense, women are the caretakers of the elderly. Men do participate in this process—some by being personal caregivers for their parents. More commonly, however, men offer services such as lawn mowing, banking, and household maintenance. Some studies have gone so far as to suggest that men spend as much time caregiving in this sense as women do. However, a difference in these two types of caregiving is that the caregiving offered by women is often required at very specific times, times over which the woman has no control. When a parent needs to go to the bathroom, the woman must drop everything and be available. The types of tasks men do can be done at the discretion of the man.

Thus, a man can plan when he will mow the lawn or balance the checkbook. This suggests that women are more likely to feel the stress of caregiving because they are at the mercy of the needs of the parent and cannot control their own schedule.

Such statistics of caregiving do not take into account the specifics of any given household. Statistically, men are more likely to marry younger women. Since women live longer than men, this combination suggests that men are more likely to receive caregiving from their wives or from their wives with the help of their children. Women, however, are more likely to outlive their husbands and thus more likely to need, and receive, help from their children. It should be noted in this context that older adults are not exclusively the receivers of caregiving from their adult children. When the literature on the exchanges between seniors and their children is examined, we find that older adults often give more than they receive, particularly in the areas of money, child care, and emotional support. One can further narrow this discussion to the particular dynamics of an individual family. All of these generalizations are useful only when they offer support for the decision-making processes of families.

When caring for an adult who has Alzheimer's disease, families need to remember that this is a progressive disease. This means that it only gets worse, never better. This means the solutions to the problems of caregiving that work today may not work tomorrow.

Experiencing Love
in the Extended Community

The role of the religious congregation in supporting families is generally as an extension of the family. Congregations may offer respite for caregivers or they may visit both the Alzheimer's-impaired person and his or her family. In this way congregations offer "gap filling" services to support the family. Just as important may be the potential for a congregation to gather resources to offer professional expertise for families. Offering support groups led by an experienced human service work or pastoral counselor who understands the issues is one important option along this line.

The congregation should be aware of the needs of families struggling to cope with caring for a loved one who has Alzheimer's disease. The congregation becomes a reflection of God's love for each person involved. This means being sensitive to the needs of the family as well as offering supportive services.

Conclusions

A cognitively impaired person is a member of a family. The nature of the disease impacts the entire family system. Families who are concerned about cognitively impaired adults need to be approached as a family, a caring unit loved by God. As families grapple with the disease, they come to learn more about themselves, as well as their friends and the members of their faith communities. Alzheimer's disease challenges everyone in our understanding of the person and the person's relationship with God. Clergy and lay leaders need to be able to support the family as they make decisions and care for the person with Alzheimer's disease.

5
Failing Brain, Faithful Community

DENISE DOMBKOWSKI HOPKINS

*I*n our search for liberating biblical texts in the struggle with Alzheimer's disease, we must listen to the voices of patients and caregivers themselves. The Bible offers many examples of honest prayer voicing the pain, anger, and doubt of people who suffer; pain is not censored or ignored. As one daughter of an Alzheimer's mother put it in a national study of stress for Alzheimer's caregivers: "What frustrates me so is that the Alzheimer's 'victims' are written off at diagnosis. They become nonpersons. People do not talk to them anymore—they talk over them or about them, etc. My mother needs peer friendships, religious opportunities. She needs people in her life besides me and the aides we hire. We are not peers; we provide care, not friendships."[1] Two books—Myrna Doernberg's *Stolen Mind* and Marion Roach's *Another Name for Madness*—written by caregivers, are such voices. Doernberg is the wife and Roach the daughter of persons with Alzheimer's.[2]

To name their own pain is to give people with Alzheimer's disease power over what is named and a sense of worth. It is to become the subject of their own experiences for as long as they can, rather than the object of someone else's view of their situation. Rev.

Failing Brain, Faithful Community

Robert Davis, who has Alzheimer's, reminds us of the disease's "hidden world": "I want to be the voice for all those victims who lost their ability to communicate."[3] Professor Cary Henderson, diagnosed with Alzheimer's at age fifty-five, notes: "I think one of the worst things about Alzheimer's is you're so alone with it. Nobody around you really knows what's going on. I would like some exchange of views, exchange of experiences, and I think for me at least, this is a very important part of life."[4]

This insistence upon letting the patients and their caregivers speak for themselves is crucial in light of psychologist Judah Ronch's observation that "Alzheimer's disease happens to people, not just to their brains." They can't "recognize a congruence with who they are and who they have been." In order to help victims find themselves, we must understand not only the level of their cognitive dysfunction, but how each person feels as well. "People do not become progressively demented without having some emotional reaction," argues Ronch. With the words of a woman named Molly about why she looked through other people's closets and drawers in the nursing home, angering the nurses and patients, Ronch illustrates his point: "I look for Molly," she said, "and I can't find her. . . . I read and don't remember. That's not me, not the real Molly. So I walk around looking for Molly, but she's nowhere to be found."[5]

Ronch has outlined six phases of a patient's subjective emotional reactions to Alzheimer's as guidelines to help caregivers focus interventions at each stage. Even in what he calls stage 6, the separation from the self, in which there is total physical dependency and no longer an active role played by the patient in his or her life environment, Ronch advises steadfast contact with "the humanness of the patient" by means of tools such as "verbal and tactile messages of concern, support, reassurance, and love." "This is a stage," Ronch says, "that no patient has ever been able to express."[6] Robert Davis anticipates the needs of this stage when he describes Alzheimer's as a "reverse aging process" that "whips us back to the place of infancy."[7] Davis

Denise Dombkowski Hopkins

describes his own special, familiar environment and established routine as his "playpen," which gradually becomes smaller and smaller as the disease progresses.

Davis also observes that "for some reason, people like us want to be touched or held. Maybe it is because we sense so many of our friends drawing back in our presence as though Alzheimer's were a communicable disease."[8] Ronch notes in this connection the "blaming the victim" responses of those who hold a "fear of senility." The "gerontophobic" behavior of some professional caregivers, the nondemented, and the elderly creates a physical and psychological distance between what they think of as "us," the healthy, and "them," the people with Alzheimer's disease.[9] Davis supports this, noting the discomfort of people around him as his diagnosis was announced. He had to seek people out who were avoiding him, declaring "I don't bite. I am still the same person. I just can't do my work anymore. . . . I need your friendship and acceptance."[10] Such attitudes and fears are nothing new. Job, too, in his response to his friends' explanations for his suffering, accused them of being afraid of what had befallen him: "You see my calamity, and are afraid. . . . But now, be pleased to look at me, for I will not lie to your face" (6:21b, 28). Fortunately, unlike Job's friends, Davis's friends expressed great relief over his words, for they "just didn't know what to say."

Psalm 41, which I have dubbed the Jerusalem hospital chaplain's psalm, vividly evokes this sense of contagion and discomfort, which is so often associated with Alzheimer's disease, by means of its open, metaphorical language. The psalmist, on her sickbed, speaks of her "enemies" in this way: "And when they come to see me, they utter empty words, while their hearts gather mischief; when they go out, they tell it abroad. All who hate me whisper together about me; they imagine the worst for me. They think that a deadly thing has fastened on me, that I will not rise again from where I lie. Even my bosom friend in whom I trusted, who ate of my bread, has lifted the heel against me. But you, O LORD, be gracious to me" (vv. 6–10). The images are painfully vivid; disease is personified as "a deadly thing" with a life of its own that threatens the healthy. How many times have people visited us in the hospital, hanging back by the door so as not to get too near and "catch" whatever it is we have, saying how great we look? We know the minute they go out the door they'll be shaking their heads and saying, "She looks like death warmed over."

There exists a dilemma for the person with Alzheimer's disease in the earlier stages of the disease, however, in connection with this issue of contagion. In the words of Robert Davis: "When I go out into society I look whole. There is no wheelchair, no bandage, or missing part to remind people of my loss. . . . For some reason some segments of society have a hard time dealing with a person who is just partly here."[11] Until well into the second stage of Alzheimer's, when things like sloppy dressing may offer clues, it is not visually obvious that anything is wrong; some Alzheimer's patients can even fool people in conversations. Davis's dilemma is exacerbated by our tendency, as a result of Cartesian dualism and the ethos of the Enlightenment and modernity, to think of ourselves primarily in terms of a mind/body split. Modernity, argues Rebecca Chopp, has divided culture into public/primary and private/secondary domains, which "are at their root gendered. The public is the domain of the man and the private is the domain of the woman."[12] The private realm encompasses "all that the public rejects: the affections, relationships, caring, and physicality," whereas the public realm is considered the realm of knowledge, objectivity, science, and power. Feminist thought has countered this tendency by lifting up the body and embodiment as marks of the human.[13]

Given this dualism, we can understand Davis's wry observation that he knew people were thinking negatively about him when he retired: "If you are unable to carry on all the responsibilities of your work, you should be bedfast or at least drooling on yourself."[14] One eight-year-old after Davis's farewell sermon even asked him why he wasn't dead yet! Also lacking is society's support for the grief process of caregivers because the one they care for doesn't look sick. This adds to

Denise Dombkowski Hopkins

their burden as they try to think for both partners in the separation process that is Alzheimer's disease.[15]

The Hebrew Bible calls us away from this kind of dualism and reminds us that humans do not simply have a body but are a body. Genesis 2:7 portrays this in striking terms: "then the LORD God formed *'adam* from the dust of the ground, and breathed into its nostrils the breath of life; and the *'adam* became a *nephesh hayyah* [a living being; a living person]." God has administered an intimate CPR to bring a lump of dust from *'adamah* (the ground), to life. English translations offer the word "soul" for the word *nephesh,* but this conjures up the body/soul dualism of the New Testament; "person" or "being" is better. *Nephesh* is not some indestructible core of being over against one's physical life that can live when cut off from that life (see also Lev. 17:10; 20:6; 22:4). In the Hebrew Bible, one's identity is encompassed within the *nephesh,* within one's being or creatureliness.

We must embrace the pain of the whole person with Alzheimer's disease as a faithful community gathered around a faithful God. We are a faithful community when we use the lament psalms to help Alzheimer's patients and caregivers speak the truth about their experience. Laments invite people to be real before a God who is with us in our reality. Picture God with big "Mickey Mouse" ears listening to our cries. We, created in God's image, need to grow our own Mickey Mouse ears to listen to one another in the community of faith. One woman on a caregivers panel for a national conference, who had cared for her mother-in-law who had Alzheimer's disease for fifteen years and is now caring for her husband, diagnosed at age fifty-four, shared that "it would have meant a lot to my husband if people said something, asked how he was. But they said nothing. He wants them to know what he's going through." Unfortunately, well-meaning people opt for silence, thinking that their questions will offend or cause the person with Alzheimer's more pain.

Israel realized the need for this sharing and listening in the book of Psalms, in which nearly one-third of the 150 psalms are laments, and of those, only seven, the so-called penitential laments (6; 32; 38; 51; 102; 130; 143), accept the experience of suffering as deserved punishment for sin. These seven are the church's Lenten favorites. The rest are angry or imprecatory laments that find the present situation of distress unfair and inexplicable and complain about it to God in the presence of the community gathered for worship.

The church, however, has not readily embraced these laments in its own worship. Responsive readings in the back of our hymnals may include laments, but usually the angry parts are cut out. Many deem the laments unchristian and are surprised to find them in the Bible at all. Why? The complaint in a lament often focuses upon one, two, or three areas: a vivid, metaphorical description of the psalmist's suffering; the "enemies" who have caused or contributed to the suffering; and God, who is accused of not caring or not doing. The first of these causes little difficulty for Christians; many of us can identify with the psalmist's descriptions, which we particularize with our own experience. The second and third, however, make many of us uncomfortable. After all, aren't we commanded by Jesus to love our enemies? Aren't accusations aimed at God blasphemy?

In fact, one pastor insists that "once you've asked the question, 'why me?' you've already lost your faith." In this view, complaining in faith is a contradiction in terms; if one complains, one cannot be faithful. Have we, as Roland Murphy wonders, "lost the art of complaining in faith to God in favor of a stoic concept of what obedience or resignation to the divine will really means"?[16] The lament is a canonical, that is, legitimate, complaint in faith to God which can be a tool for the faithful community in dealing with Alzheimer's disease. The focus of the Hebrew Bible is this-worldly, and consequently the pain of the person with Alzheimer's disease is honored by the lament psalms. The urgency of lament language reminds us that the pain of this life cannot be too easily dismissed by a belief in life after death which will put everything right.

Robert Davis includes several laments in his autobiography.

Denise Dombkowski Hopkins

During the time when doctors were searching for a diagnosis and his memory was slipping more and more, Davis panicked over his relationship to God: "I could only cry out bitterly to the Lord, 'Why God, why? How can you leave me at a time like this? . . . O God, I have lost so much already!'" He continued to lament once the diagnosis was made: "At those times I would weep and cry out to God, 'Why, God, why?' . . . What did I ever do to deserve this?"[17] Similarly, his wife, Betty, in the epilogue to Davis's book, writes with eloquent pain: "Sometimes in weakness and despair I want to give voice to that primal scream starting way down in the hidden recesses of the lungs—down where the ever-present knot that lives in my stomach resides—let it whirl through that vortex that's sucking my life and being into the black hole of never-ending pain, emptiness, and loneliness—just give it voice as it rises and explodes through the top of my head—Nooooooo! No, God, no! Not us! Not this! Not his mind! Not his personhood! Anything, God, but this!"[18]

Just as in the biblical lament psalms, Betty and Bob's laments begin with an address to God, packed with emotion, identifying the One to whom the psalmist prays, even claiming a past relationship—"my God"—and then moving quickly into the complaint word "why." "Why?" was a question I hurled at God unceasingly after my twenty-three-year-old brother inexplicably drowned. Many caregivers ask "Why? Why?" for many years after the diagnosis of a loved one, and are angry at God. Psalm 22:1, taken up by Jesus on the cross (Matt. 27:46 and Mark 15:34), showcases the "Why?" question: "My God, my God, why have you forsaken me?" The Hebrew question *lamah* ("Why?") is the most frequently occurring question in the lament psalms. We make a mistake to think that when someone in pain voices these questions, they want information, that is, God did this because . . . Or, in response to another lament question, How long? we answer three weeks, or two years, as if the pain could be explained away in this way. As one caregiver said about his father with Alzheimer's: "Don't say it will be all right. It won't. I want you to understand what we're going through."

This is what Job's friends tried to do in response to Job's bitter questions, and this is what Job reacted angrily against. As Harold Kushner rightly notes in *When Bad Things Happen to Good People:* "In reality, Job's words were not a theological question at all, but a cry of pain."[19] The best thing that Job's friends did for him was to sit in silence with him for seven days and seven nights; in this they showed pastoral solidarity. They became tormentors when they opened their mouths and started talking theology. The friends sitting in silence paid attention to what Daniel Simundson calls the "survival" or "gut" level of suffering, that is, God's presence with the sufferer through the friends. When they moved to theologizing, they dealt with Job's suffering on the intellectual level, which was much easier for them, but which distanced Job and the friends from God's presence in Job's suffering.[20] Here, then, in the response of Job's friends, is a pastoral model for how *not* to deal with the suffering of Alzheimer's disease.

Bob's and Betty's questions of "Why me?" and "Why us?" are undergirded by the theory of act/consequence and the KINGAFAP image of God. As Brian Wren describes it, the KINGAFAP metaphor system offers the King-God-Almighty-Father-Protector, the monarch who rules alone in control of everything, mirroring the domination of males over females in society.[21] Such a metaphor system undergirds the strong thread of act/consequence or divine retribution running throughout the entire Bible; a powerful God rewards the righteous and punishes the wicked.[22] "Why me?" means "What did I do to deserve this?"

In the wisdom tradition of Israel, this kind of thinking is encapsulated in the theme of the Two Ways, summed up by the proverb verse in Psalm 1:6: "For the LORD watches over the way of the righteous, but the way of the wicked will perish." The way of the righteous leads to reward and life, while the way of the wicked leads to punishment and death (cf. Prov. 11:17, 31, etc.). Prophecies of disaster are based upon this principle of act/consequence, as for example, in Micah 6:9–13: "The voice of the LORD cries to the city. . . . Your wealthy are full of violence;

your inhabitants speak lies. . . . *Therefore* I have begun to strike you down, making you desolate because of your sins." The prophets connect the sin and disobedience of the people with the coming judgment, with exile. The whole Deuteronomistic History (Joshua, Judges, 1 and 2 Samuel, and 1 and 2 Kings) views Israel's history as reward and punishment based upon its actions. The book of Deuteronomy sets before the Israelites the choice about covenanting: to obey the commandments means life, but to disobey means death—a choice made especially clear in Deuteromy 30:15–20. The New Testament picks up this theme in many places: Matthew 7:17: You will know them by their fruits; Galatians 6:7–10: God is not mocked, for whatever one sows, that one will also reap; Matthew 7:13–14: Many enter the wide gate to destruction, but few enter the narrow gate to life, and so on. This theme of act/consequence runs like a thread through the entire Bible.

The problem with this way of thinking is that we can easily victimize the victim. This is because when we work backward from the consequence, that is, from sickness or material success or whatever, we tend to focus on it as a consequence, rather than on the act or condition itself and what caused it.[23] Job's friends did this. They automatically assumed that he had done something to deserve his suffering. Consequently, they could not listen sympathetically to Job's pain for longer than seven days and nights. God looms as the punisher God; God's grace is eclipsed by God's judgment. The result of this kind of thinking can only be despair and a sense of isolation for the Alzheimer's victim.

Cultural assumptions about health exacerbate this problem of act/consequence. We believe we can stay young forever and avoid death by exercising, eating right, wearing the right clothes, and so on. If we play by all the rules, Alzheimer's shouldn't exist. In this "Prozac society" of ours, as the *Washington Post* put it recently, "our dominant cultural institutions, from high schools to ad agencies—celebrate a notion of 'personality' that is upbeat, sociable and energetic."[24] Pop an Advil and your headache flees in thirty seconds. Sitcoms and Dear

Abby can solve our most gut-wrenching problems in no time at all. There is no room for Alzheimer's in such a world. The public domain in which we live values production and exchange. The body is viewed as a machine that must be maintained to keep up its production. There is no room for Alzheimer's in this world either. Bob Davis felt this keenly: "In Alzheimer's disease there is the loss of the personality, a diminished sense of self-worth. A highly productive person has to wonder why he is still alive and what purpose the Lord has in keeping him on this earth. As I struggle with the indignities that accompany daily living, I am losing my sense of humanity and self-worth."[25]

The church, sharing in these cultural assumptions, has responded to the aging process in different ways. One response is to create "all kinds of programs designed to keep aging persons involved."[26] Older people are supposed to keep busy with crafts, lunches, trips, and volunteerism to hold their aging at bay. Alzheimer's patients eventually can't keep up. This increases their sense of isolation and despair. Judah Ronch criticizes this approach. It is not enough, he says, to keep the patient busy at a minimum level of competency, which can be demoralizing. Things must be done to perpetuate the "I" and "allow continuity of self-identity in the midst of cognitive decline."[27] At the other extreme, the church's response has been a "guided disengagement" expressed in media programs, telephone contacts, counseling, and lay/pastoral visitation, which leave older people alone most of the time, except for a voice over the telephone and one or two people from church who visit occasionally. The goal is disengagement from this world to prepare for death.[28] This kind of isolation can be frightening and depressing for people with Alzheimer's disease.

Returning to the theme of act/consequence, it must be noted that we don't consciously think about act/consequence in our day-to-day living, especially when things are going well for us. But as soon as something goes wrong, this thinking surfaces in our question, Why me? The faithful community needs to understand these dynamics when people with Alzheimer's disease

Denise Dombkowski Hopkins

and their caregivers give vent to their anger and frustration. For as Ronch argues, the question "Why me?" will surface. At what Ronch calls phase 3 of six stages of emotional reactions to the experience of Alzheimer's the patient incorporates "the fact of being demented into the patient's self-representation and into the world of his/her future."[29] This means that caregivers and counselors must deal with the patient's shock, confusion, guilt, sadness, and rage, and with questions about what the person did to cause the disease.

Cary Henderson illustrates this stage when he writes:

> I think that this disease does make us kind of irrational—and sometimes it's out of fear and sometimes it's being left out of things. . . . I do think it's bad that we sometimes become almost afraid of ourselves and almost afraid of our caregivers and our family. . . . I think for a lot of us the feeling of being cheated or belittled and somehow made jokes of, I think that's one thing that is among the worst things about Alzheimer's.[30]

This is true for caregivers as well as persons with Alzheimer's disease.

Bob Davis's descriptions of his suffering with Alzheimer's correspond to the complaint section of the lament psalms. Just as the psalmist in Psalm 77:4 complains to God that "You keep my eyelids from closing" and in Psalm 6:6 proclaims: "I am weary with my moaning; every night I flood my bed with tears," Davis speaks repeatedly of his problems with falling asleep, describing the terror of it in the vivid, metaphorical language that the psalmists use: "There was nothing there. This vacuum was filled with terrifying blackness." Describing how he soaked his bed with sweat in response to the terror of monsters that sometimes filled the blackness, he wrote: "When the darkness and emptiness fill my mind, it is totally terrifying. I cannot think my way out of it. . . . The only way I can break this cycle is to move."[31] This helps to explain the wandering that is characteristic of Alzheimer's patients in the second stage of the disease.

Psalm 88 seems to capture the chaos, confusion, and terror

of Bob Davis's nights: "O LORD, . . . when, at night, I cry out in your presence, let my prayer come before you" (vv. 1–2). The psalmist describes her or his suffering in terms of death, the power of darkness, and going down to Sheol or the Pit, that place in the bowels of the earth where the dead go to exist as shades of their former selves: "For my *nephesh* is full of troubles, and my life draws near to Sheol. I am counted among those who go down to the Pit . . . like those whom you remember no more, for they are cut off from your hand. You have put me in the depths of the Pit" (vv. 3–6). The sufferer may not actually be close to death, not on her or his deathbed per se, but anything that threatens the *shalom* or wholeness of the psalmist—whether loss of memory, social isolation, or disease—is likened to death and makes one feel as good as dead. As Bob Davis contends, "I believe that the death of the real individual sometimes comes even before his physical death comes. . . . Alzheimer's kills all that is truly me while it turns the rest of my brain to mush."[32]

Another dimension of the lament psalms worth noting, because it has a bearing on the dignity of the patient and caregiver, can be called the "PR value" of the psalmist.[33] The psalmist reminds God that she or he can be a valuable public relations agent for God, witnessing to others about God's saving acts. In the lament psalm, just in case God was not moved by the vivid, metaphorical descriptions of the psalmist's suffering and enemies, the psalmist provides several motivations, in addition to the public relations argument, for God's answering the petitions. The most familiar motivation is the confession of sin. Another, the protestation of innocence, is problematic, because it maintains that suffering is not justified and therefore help is due. An example is Psalm 17:3: "You have tested my heart . . . you will find no wickedness in me."

A third motivation is the public relations argument. If God allows the psalmist to die and go down to Sheol, then calling upon God and God's answering are not possible, and neither is praising God for deliverance, as the psalmist does in Psalm 30:1: "I will extol you, *Adonai*, for you have lifted me up." God will lose out on the psalmist's praise. As Psalm 6:5 reminds God: "In death there is no remembrance of you; in Sheol who can praise you?" I do not mean to support the hope for miraculous healing by raising this issue. I do want to emphasize that what is most importantly at stake in this idea of the PR value is the value of the psalmist. The psalmist matters to God. For "the speaker is *valued by God* as one who praises," Walter Brueggemann tells us in *The Message of the Psalms*.[34] A kind of parity is assumed in the relationship. This argument by the psalmists places them within the *chutzpah* tradition of the Hebrew Bible, that is, "boldness with regard to heaven."[35] This tradition is found not only in the psalms, but also in narrative prayers such as Genesis 18:23–33, with Abraham arguing with God over the fate of Sodom; Jacob wrestling at the Jabbok in Genesis 32:9–12; Moses interceding for the people after the golden calf incident in Exodus 32, and so on.[36]

Because God is a God who hears and because God values us as someone who matters, we are freed to be as honest with God as we can in prayer. There is thus no need for caregivers to "pretty up their prayers" before such a God, especially when it comes to the issue of "ledger balancing," that is, of reciprocating to the parent with Alzheimer's "in an identical way for the care given to him/her as a child." The laments can reassure caregiver children that "the invisible loyalties that contain them are part of a contract they did not knowingly sign, and that having angry feelings about a relative does not mean one doesn't love him/her."[37] God "hears us into speech" as Nelle Morton puts it, whatever that speech is, thereby cleansing us of emotions that can only fester and hurt us.[38]

In this way, Job's wife urges Job "to curse God and die" (Job 1:9). Job rebukes her as a foolish woman. The Septuagint gives her a longer speech in which she speaks of Job's sufferings and her own, as does the *Testament of Job*, but these make her a more sympathetic character and her words more excusable. Carol Newsom suggests that we reject these expansions and acknowledge that it is Job's wife who is "the one who recognizes . . . long before Job himself does, what is at stake theologically in innocent suffering: the conflict between innocence and integrity, on the one hand, and an affirmation of the goodness of God, on the other." Her "iconoclastic words" are condemned defensively but serve "as an irritant that undermines old complacencies."[39]

A text from 2 Samuel 12:20–23 dealing with the illness of David's son from his illicit union with Bathsheba helps us understand another aspect of the grieving process of spouses of people with Alzheimer's disease. One such spouse wrote, "When Al died, I had no more need to grieve. I was relieved. . . . But while he was alive, I grieved every day."[40] In the same way, King David fasts and weeps and prays while his child struggles for life, but as soon as the child died, David washed, changed his clothes, worshiped, and ate, to his servants' amazement. He said, "While the child was still alive, I fasted and wept; for I said, 'Who knows? The LORD may be gracious to me, and the child may live.' But now he is dead; why should I fast? Can I bring him back again?" (vv. 22–23). This text can help those of us interacting with caregivers put their grief in a more understandable perspective.

It is not enough for the rabbi or pastor or counselor or caregiver alone to work through the pain of a person with Alzheimer's disease. Without the support of the larger community of faith that care will be helpful but incomplete. Robert Davis knows this. He knows that his mind's assurances of God's promises and presence will cease as the disease progresses. "Then," he says, "I must rely solely on those who love me to keep me close to the Father by their prayers, and to reassure me with songs and touch and simple words of Scripture."[41] Ronch observes that in phase 5 of a patient's emotional reaction to Alzheimer's, special bonds of maturation are created with caregivers and that people with Alzheimer's "can be made to feel less anxious if they are part of something more continuous than their own fragmented existence."[42] Our shared human vulnerability can help to create a bond of interdependency and connnectedness.

The community of faith needs to take up the role of an Elijah or a Jeremiah, suffering with the suffering and going up against God, if need be, on their behalf. First Kings 17 shows us this clearly. Elijah is sent to the widow of Zeraphath, who is starving during the famine God has sent. She and her household are able to eat because of Elijah's presence. But the widow's son becomes ill and dies. The widow accuses Elijah of coming "to bring my sin to remembrance, and to cause the death of my son" (v. 18). Elijah challenges God in verse 20: "O LORD my God, have you brought calamity even upon the widow with whom I am staying, by killing her son?"[43] In Jeremiah 4, the prophet (or is it God the divine self?) experiences and feels the pain that is to come upon the sinful people Israel. He moans, "My anguish, my anguish! I writhe in pain! . . . I looked on the earth, and lo, it was waste and void. . . . I looked, and lo, there was no one at all" (vv. 19, 23, 25). This is incarnational presence with those who suffer.

Samuel Balentine argues just this point: "When the church takes seriously the practice of lament, it affirms that in a suffering world God is on the side of the victim. If any word from God is to be spoken in the face of suffering, it must be articulated from the standpoint of the victim, not the onlooker."[44] The "primal screams" of people with Alzheimer's will and must always shake our theology. "Such cries of anguish," insists Balentine, "belong in the sanctuary; to put the matter more directly, the church must be sanctuary in the midst of the cries of anguish." Otherwise there will only be room in church for Job's friends, who are too eager for intellectual explanations of suffering. This ministry of the church "will always place the church at the side of Job, where to be faithful to God is to speak pain *with,* if not like, the victim."[45] In this way, the church most clearly embodies divine compassion; shattering questions keep hope alive, even in despair.

Glenn Weaver argues similarly that a resurrection theology for dementia should include assurances that people with dementia remain one with the whole body of Christ. He argues that "churches should make provisions for patients to attend services as long as they possibly can," and when that is no longer possible, they should be visited at home by "a core group of familiar

Failing Brain, Faithful Community

members who are well-versed" in Alzheimer's strategies. Weaver reminds us that "memory is a social experience."[46] We negotiate our memory of the past in our conversations with one another. Robert Davis expresses this view poignantly: "I want to shout, 'Be gentle with your loved ones. Listen to them. Hear their whispered pain. Touch them. Include them in activity meaningful to them. Help them stay in touch with God. Let them draw from your strength.'"[47]

Bruce Birch notes the three roles the community of faith can play in a crisis like Alzheimer's disease.[48] First, it can relieve isolation. Second, it can hold up the symbols of our faith so that they are available to us in time of trauma, symbols such as "exodus" and "resurrection," not to obscure death and pain, but to show that these are not the last word. Third, the community of faith can mediate the healing word by receiving our pain and loss and looking to "a further word of meaning."

Perry LeFevre has conceived a theology for what he calls the "helpless aged" such as persons with Alzheimer's disease. How can their lives have a clear direction with Christ as the goal? He warns that we cannot know by appearances alone "what dimensions of centeredness, freedom, or responsive love have been lost even in the most debilitated persons. . . . Essential humanness . . . can transcend speech and have forms of expression that are deeper than word and concept. . . . Love is social. . . . It is *both* a giving and a receiving."[49]

His hopeful word is that "the fragile and dependent elderly, even those who are confused and senile, have not lost all center. To be a center is *not only* to give but to receive, and those who cannot yet give—the new born child, or those who can no longer give, may yet give, in *receiving* care."[50] They give in their receiving, by being open to caring love. This is a "profound symbol of the ultimate human condition before God" even for those of us in full health. Our capacity to give and to care rests on another, the Divine Spirit. For Bob Davis, loss of self-confidence and pride accompanied his journey into Alzheimer's disease, as he became "a care receiver instead of a care giver."[51] LeFevre's view puts that move into a new and hopeful light.

6
Hope:
The Community Looks Forward

STEPHEN SAPP

*W*ill Rogers once said, "Everything is funny—as long as it happens to somebody else." If that is true, then growing old must not be so funny because, although it is unquestionably happening to everybody else, it is just as certainly happening to each individual observing them as well. In fact, it is currently happening to more and more people in this country, leading to much rhetoric about the "graying of America." One result of this universal human experience of growing old is that at some point many people will no longer be able to take care of themselves and will need some level of assistance before they die. Indeed, according to Carl Eisdorfer, chair of psychiatry at the University of Miami School of Medicine and one of the founders of what is now the national Alzheimer's Association, for every five years one lives past the age of sixty-five, the amount of care the person needs doubles.[1]

The incidence of Alzheimer's disease also increases significantly with age. Some authorities even estimate that half of those who live to be eighty-five will develop the disease by then. Given that the fastest-growing segment of the United States population is those who are now eighty-five and older, the importance of the subject of this book to leaders of religious institutions is obvious.

Hope: The Community Looks Forward

When the great French actor/singer Maurice Chevalier was asked how he felt about aging, he is said to have responded, "Growing old isn't so bad—when you consider the alternative." With the lengthening of the life span, however, and thus the increased likelihood of living long enough to face the prospect of Alzheimer's disease, if not in oneself then in a loved one, more and more people are beginning to feel that perhaps the alternative to getting *that* old is actually preferable. In an undergraduate bioethics class at the University of Miami the high incidence of Alzheimer's disease in those over eighty-five was mentioned, and one of the senior students (who was twenty-one years old) immediately responded, "I'm going to die before I get that old." When asked if she were serious or just being flip, she said, with no hint of a smile on her face, "I'm completely serious."

This incident calls to mind the story of the two physicians riding together to a medical society meeting. One said, "I bet we have roast beef, baked potatoes with butter and sour cream, and something like cheesecake for dessert. With all we know about fat, cholesterol, and their link to stroke and heart disease, you'd think a medical association would choose banquet menus more carefully." His friend agreed, and their conversation turned to other matters, including the increase in dementing illnesses with the aging of the United States population. They began to share experiences they had had with persons with Alzheimer's disease and their families. When they got to the banquet both of them asked for seconds on the prime rib, butter, and cheesecake!

What can keep people from adopting such an attitude of resignation, if not outright despair, especially if they are dealing with a dementing illness in either themselves or a loved one? One of the best antidotes available, if not the best, is the subject of this chapter, *hope*—certainly something about which the Western religious tradition has a great deal to say. As in the exploration of memory in chapter 3, this chapter will utilize a twofold approach to the topic: first a consideration of the more individual, personal dimensions, and then a look at some corporate or communal aspects.

Stephen Sapp

Personal Dimensions

When a person has Alzheimer's disease, in addition to the practical matters that must be dealt with, two critical questions arise: first, the relationship of God to creation in general and to human beings in particular, and second, as chapter 3 suggested, the nature of the person. In this regard, David Keck rightly observes that Alzheimer's disease raises "theological and ecclesiological problems . . . of enormous significance for all of us since they strike at the heart of who we are and what we may become." Indeed, he goes so far as to label Alzheimer's the "Theological Disease."[2] Thus theology is a useful vehicle for exploring the issues that often trouble people with dementia, at least early on, and that certainly bedevil family members throughout the illness (and even afterward).

In chapter 3 the theological dimensions of Alzheimer's disease were approached from a rather eclectic theological perspective. Ultimately, however, if one is to claim that religious traditions have anything to offer in dealing with Alzheimer's disease, one's own particular theological position must be brought to bear upon whatever insights can be gained about the issue under consideration. Thus in this chapter the question of hope in the face of dementia will be approached from the particular faith perspective of the Reformed tradition. In doing so, the focus will be on the thought of the formative figure in that tradition, John Calvin. Despite his "peculiarities," however, Calvin is representative enough of Protestant Christianity in general that his ideas are translatable into other theological traditions.

Calvin

John Calvin was a sixteenth-century French lawyer turned Protestant reformer who spent much of his career in Geneva. Thus he lived almost four hundred years before the medical description of Alzheimer's disease was articulated. Although it seems highly likely that some persons during Calvin's time must have been cognitively impaired, Calvin never wrote directly about this problem (though he would no doubt happily have affirmed that a number of the people he encountered in Geneva were demented—a diagnosis they no doubt would have reciprocated). Because he did not address the issue, we can only infer from other aspects of Calvin's writing what he might have said about this particular malady. Still, as with any theology (or system of thought of any kind) that is being applied to a time and place unknown to its author, it is possible to strive to be faithful to the thought of that person in the attempt to arrive at a picture of how he or she might have addressed such a topic. At the very least, one can try to glean from the person's work insights that are applicable even in today's different world.

Mary Potter Engel notes that Calvin is "a theocentric Christian theologian *par excellence*," meaning that everything he says and everything he advocates as proper human action reflect first and foremost the grandeur and glory of God.[3] As Calvin asserts in his magnum opus, the *Institutes of the Christian Religion*, "Now the great thing is this: we are consecrated and dedicated to God in order that we may thereafter think, speak, meditate, and do, nothing except to his glory. . . . We are God's: let us therefore live for him and die for him."[4] This emphasis by Calvin on the *sola gloria Dei* can at first seem to render his theology less useful in situations such as the topic of this book than, say, a contemporary approach like process theology, which appears to be much more concerned with things human.

Calvin, however, would not have agreed, and he was determined to assure that knowledge of God and knowledge of humanity always be kept together, though priority of course remained with the former. The very first words of the *Institutes* make this point clearly: "Nearly all the wisdom we possess, that is to say, true and sound wisdom, consists of two parts: the knowledge of God and of ourselves" (1.1.1). Indeed, it is only through knowledge of God that human beings can come truly to know themselves, for at least two reasons. First, humans are created in the image of God, and it is impossible truly to know the likeness without knowing the reality it reflects. As Calvin puts it, "It is certain that man never achieves a clear knowledge of himself unless he has first looked upon God's face, and then descends from contemplating him to scrutinize himself" (1.1.2).

The second reason one must know God in order to know oneself is that secular self-knowledge tends to promote pride, whereas self-knowledge that comes from first knowing the grandeur of God calls forth a response of humility by reminding human beings of their creaturehood. As just one example of this point, Calvin urges his readers to raise their thoughts to God and to ponder God's "nature, and how completely perfect are his righteousness, wisdom, and power" because these are "the straightedge to which we must be shaped." Then we will come to realize that "what in us seems perfection itself corresponds ill to the purity of God" (1.2.2). At the same time, however, this approach precludes despair or denigration of one's humanity because humans are after all creatures of God, who is all-wise and therefore must have known what God was doing when God created humankind. This radically theocentric approach of Calvin offers a rich source of hope in several ways for those touched by Alzheimer's disease.

Perhaps the first thing to learn from Calvin's thought is an important reminder to those who do *not* suffer from cognitive impairment. He makes quite clear in many places in his writings that *all* human beings are impaired when it comes to any of the natural faculties because of the role sin plays in each human life and in the history of the human race; this of course is the famous (some would say infamous) doctrine of *total depravity* (which affirms not that there is no good at all in human beings, but that there is not one aspect of human existence that is not distorted and degraded by the effects of sin). It is only God's grace that overcomes the depravity all humans bear as a result of the sin of Adam.

In fact, because of the ubiquitous effects of sin in human life, it can truly be said that all human beings suffer from a form of "spiritual Alzheimer's disease." That is, they are always *forget-*

ting God and God's saving work on their behalf, and they seldom *remember* to give God the glory for all the things they think they accomplish on their own. Furthermore, the prayers and actions of a given person are, in God's sight, often as incoherent and pointless as are the words and deeds of demented individuals to that person.

By starting from divine nature instead of human nature, then, Calvin's approach renders much less important the standards that human beings constantly try to bring to bear upon variously impaired persons in order to determine their "humanhood." These criteria include reason, self-direction, ability to relate to others, and so forth, all of which are progressively lost in dementing illnesses.[5] So before people judge the capacities of persons with cognitive impairments too harshly, Calvin might caution them to look first to their own particular impairments.

This discussion calls to mind another important concept in Calvin's thought. Although his view of *imago Dei*—human creation in the image of God—is too complex to examine in detail, this doctrine, which once again is rooted in Calvin's theocentric understanding of all reality, also contributes to a sense of hope in the context of Alzheimer's disease. For Calvin, the image of God in humans is in no way a *natural* endowment, a possession that belongs to human beings in any sort of intrinsic way, as a birthright that comes simply because of membership in the species *Homo sapiens*. Rather, God's image in humans consists in *God's* beholding, that is, in God's seeing God's self reflected in these particular creatures, so to speak. Thus the image really comes into full existence only through the obedient and faithful response of humans to God's gracious initiative. That is, the *more* God sees God's self reflected in humans, the better they demonstrate the image of God in which they are created.

The problem, of course, is that sin has distorted human ability to render this response, though it has not destroyed it altogether (*Institutes* 1.15.4). The "mirror" is still there, but it has become like a fun-house mirror, or maybe better, a "tragic-house" mirror. As

Stephen Sapp

Thomas F. Torrance interprets Calvin's view, "The *imago dei* must be understood teleologically and eschatologically, for it is only shadowed forth in man until he reaches perfection." The image of God, therefore, is "man's destiny in God's gracious intention. It is the original truth of his being which is also future."[6] In short, *no* human being reflects God's image perfectly; that possibility was lost in the original disobedience. The atoning work of Jesus Christ, however, restores at least the possibility of doing so, but only when humans reach perfection.

Again, those who are cognitively unimpaired are reminded not to make judgments about those with cognitive impairments without realizing that those judgments may well apply to themselves as well. Furthermore, if even sin cannot destroy the *imago Dei*, then it would appear that a disease process certainly cannot do so. By keeping the focus clearly on God and God's glory, Calvin's theology affirms that even in a cognitively impaired state, the individual can still reflect that glory, surely a cause for hope.

More specifically, in his insistence on starting with God, Calvin makes it clear that it is always God who comes to human beings, not vice versa. If this is the case, then does it matter what condition a person is in if *God* chooses to come? As the discussion above demonstrated, if God had not chosen to come to humankind in the person of Jesus Christ despite the impairments all humans suffer because of their sin, every human being who has ever lived would be utterly lost.

Furthermore, what evidence really exists that God does *not* still come to those who are cognitively impaired? The widely held assumption that a person's capacity to relate to God is lost when he or she loses cognitive function may just sell *God* short. Unless one's ability to relate to God is equated with one's mind (rational and conscious mind, at that, which is a very dangerous and non-Christian attitude[7]), the view that God no longer relates to the person with advanced dementia may simply be the imposition of post-Enlightenment psychology onto the person with Alzheimer's disease.

That is, contemporary American culture seems increasingly

to think that if an organism lacks the ability to engage in rational thought, that organism is of little value, certainly of less value than "rational" creatures. This point of view may even go so far as to question the "real" humanity of such a being, an attitude that is distinctly nonbiblical (see chapter 3). Calvin's emphasis on God's taking the initiative to come to humankind, whatever the level or type of impairment a given individual suffers, is therefore a welcome corrective. It offers hope that despite the dementia, God can still relate to a person even if his or her ability to relate to God (or to other people) appears lost. It is arguable, in fact, that *every* human's ability to relate to God is blocked by sin just as effectively as most people assume that of a person with Alzheimer's is blocked by loss of cognitive function. But if God can and does still come to human beings even through their sin, then . . .

Calvin's radically theocentric perspective can serve to keep ever in view another critical point in attempting to find some hope in the face of a disease like Alzheimer's, namely, that human beings are totally dependent upon God and can achieve nothing on their own merit. As Calvin says, God "accepts us as the work of His hand. Then we must not pretend to be loved at God's hand for any deserts of our own, but because He sees we are His workmanship."[8] It is the consistent witness of the Jewish and Christian faiths, which Calvin reflects, that human beings are incapable of saving themselves. Only as God intervenes (through the giving of Torah in Judaism or the incarnation in Christianity) can the relationship between God and God's human creatures be restored. This reliance on the freely given grace of God—"justification by grace through faith," *the* central doctrine of the Protestant Reformation—is perhaps the hardest thing that human beings have to learn. It is probably also the reason that residents of the United States of America especially—with their highly developed sense of individualism, self-reliance, and belief that one is what one achieves—have so much trouble facing up to growing older: As people age, they become more and more dependent and less and less able to maintain the facade that they are really independent and in total control of their own destiny. This point is relevant, incidentally, to the desire on the part of some persons with Alzheimer's disease to commit suicide before they are "too far gone": they just cannot face the loss of their individuality and autonomy, with the accompanying prospect of dependence.[9]

This increased dependence is simply not a problem for Calvin because he knows from the outset that he is not his own master, the creator of his own life and destiny, but precisely a creature of the sovereign God who in mercy has ordered all things for the best. All human beings depend for their existence entirely on God's grace; they have not been given a bit of God in their souls, nor is the soul in any sense a transfusion of God into the human being (*Institutes* 1.15.5). The bottom line is that if God were to withdraw God's sustaining Spirit for a moment, human beings would return to the nothingness from which they were called into existence by that same loving God (*creatio ex nihilo;* "creation out of nothing"). Indeed, all creation owes its existence in every moment to the gracious will of God.

More specifically for the concerns of this chapter, if such utter dependence on the grace of God holds true for *all* human beings, it narrows the gap considerably between the cognitively impaired and the cognitively unimpaired (*relatively* unimpaired, that is, or, as Daniel Callahan once felicitously put it, the "currently sound-minded and able-bodied"). Just as Calvin's emphasis on the doctrine of total depravity affirms that all human beings are impaired in some way, so if all are also totally dependent, then the difference between the person with Alzheimer's disease and the caregiver is merely a matter of degree, not substance! A recognition of their own undeniable dependence upon God's grace thus can serve to make those in caregiving roles more sensitive to and appreciative of the needs of the person with dementia because, in a very real sense according to Calvin, there *in* the grace of God go they! Such a view can also perhaps help those with Alzheimer's in the early stages of the illness to accept that they are not so radically different from their caregivers.

Corporate Dimensions

This discussion of human beings' fundamental dependence upon God (and ultimately upon other people in old age) suggests another aspect of Calvin's theological anthropology that can be instructive when we attempt to understand how to approach the topic of hope in relation to Alzheimer's disease. Here the individual perspective of the discussion up to this point yields again to the corporate in a consideration of Calvin's view of the communal nature of the Christian life and the place of believers within the body of Christ.

The third book of the *Institutes* deals with the Holy Spirit's work in the heart of the individual believer. After Calvin reaffirms "our ignorance and (sloth to which I add fickleness of disposition)," he uses the fourth book to present his doctrine of the church, which he says God has given to humankind as one of the "outward helps to beget and increase faith within us, and advance it to its goal" (4.1.1). Because of the theocentrism of Calvin's scheme, the two books hang together quite naturally: The major emphasis is neither the place of the individual nor the role of the community but always the redeeming grace of God, a grace that calls the individual to new life, yet only as it is lived in the community of faith. Indeed, as John Leith points out, Calvin's theology does "not distinguish between an individual Christianity and a communal Christianity." Thus "in addition to the emphasis on moral and spiritual growth, the human response to God's grace that constitutes the Christian life is also typified by its communal character. The Christian life takes place in the Christian community and . . . [its] source and strength are derived from the body of Christ." [10] Calvin's use of the organic imagery of the body means that he sees the church as more than just a voluntary association of people: Christians are not a "civil society, but, being ingrafted into Christ's body, are truly members one of another."[11]

This emphasis in Calvin's theology lends support to the place of the person with dementia within the community of believers as suggested in chapter 3: Every Christian has a place within the body of Christ, especially as life comes to a close. Because Christians are collectively the body of Christ, if an individual's memory is lost, the body can remember for that person. If personal cognitive function begins to fade, the body can declare the faith together for that person, who is an organic member of the *one body* that Christ's church represents. If individual identity is collapsing, the body of Christ can uphold that person and all those who live in hope of the resurrection. Incidentally, on a practical level, this concept also argues strongly for the church's active involvement in caring not only for persons with dementia but also for their caregivers, an area in which it currently falls woefully short.

Calvin's discussion of three particular aspects of the communion that is the church suggests that he would agree with the approach that is being outlined here. First and not surprisingly, Christ is the head of the body and the source of "all the vigor" that the church possesses: "All the life or health which is diffused through the members flows from the head." The second aspect, though, speaks more directly to the point just made: "By the distribution [of Christ's gifts] made, the limited share of each [member] renders the communication between all the members absolutely necessary." That is, the divine gifts are spread among all the members of the body (recall 1 Corinthians 12), and thus if the body is to function as intended, those gifts must be shared in mutually beneficial ways.[12] Finally,

> without mutual love, the health of the body cannot be maintained. Through the members, as canals, is conveyed from the head all that is necessary for the nourishment of the body. While this connection is upheld, the body is alive and healthy. Each member, too, has its own proper share, according to the effectual working in the measure of every part (*CR* 51:203).

The implications of such an approach for the care of cognitively impaired persons are profound. Clearly the interdependence of the members of the body of Christ is crucial for Calvin, in contrast to the independence so fostered by contemporary society. In words directly applicable to caring for persons with

Alzheimer's disease, Calvin affirms that "no one has so much as to have enough within himself, so as not to require help from others." The Spirit of God distributes gifts to each in such a way that no one receives all, "lest anyone, satisfied with his particular portion, should separate himself from others and live solely for himself" (*CR* 49:500). Even more pointedly, he asserts that "no member of the body of Christ is endowed with such perfection as to be able, without the assistance of others, to supply his own necessities" (*CR* 51:192). Once again Calvin's theology suggests that differences between impaired and unimpaired individuals may be more a matter of degree than substance. No human being, however unimpaired in his or her own view, can make it alone, without the assistance of others.

Interestingly, in speaking of schism within the body of Christ, Calvin wrote against the Anabaptists: "This should serve as a warning to us that when under the guise of a zeal for perfection, we are not able to bear any imperfection either in the body or in the members of the church, it is the devil who inflames us with pride and seduces us by hypocrisy" (*CR* 7:77). Given his organic view of the church, in which all believers are truly one with Christ and with one another, it seems reasonable to apply this statement to our attitude toward persons with dementia, who manifestly show "imperfection." The basic depravity of all humans, coupled with the warning just quoted, should serve as a vivid reminder to those who might be tempted to think less of people with cognitive impairment.

Ossie Davis, the respected actor, told a story at a meeting of the American Society on Aging that illustrates beautifully the communal relationship of interdependence that Calvin argues is demanded by the Christian faith, a relationship that can give hope to those both young and old:

> A group of Jews fleeing Germany during the Holocaust had to cross a mountain to reach safety. Some of the older members of the group began to tire and asked to be left behind to fend for themselves rather than endanger everybody else by slowing them down. A number of the younger people, fearing for their

own safety, were quite ready to agree. A wise younger person in the group, however, countered by saying, "We realize that you are old, tired, and infirm, and that you just want to sit down and rest. But we have these young women with babies, and they are so tired from carrying them this far. Will each of you older people take a baby and just carry it as far as you can before you give out? Then we'll leave you there." Everybody in the group made it across the mountain!

This story illustrates what younger people can offer to those who are older, namely, a sense of purpose, of being needed, of having something to contribute. But the story also demonstrates quite well the mutuality that can stem from a recognition that all are impaired in some way and thus dependent upon God's mercy and one another's caring concern if anyone is to make it through the "vale of tears" that is human life in a fallen world. Regardless of age, all persons have certain claims upon one another. But everyone also has certain responsibilities as well. Certainly the Christian message is unequivocally that the lives of all are enhanced when all are willing to give of themselves for the good of the whole.

I want to conclude this chapter on a somewhat personal note. As I reflected on its subject—hope—a perhaps unusual link formed in my mind between two seemingly unrelated natural phenomena. The first of course is the focus of this book: Alzheimer's disease. The second is an experience I had in August 1992 that will color the way I see reality for a long time to come, as it will for all those who shared that experience with me. Category 4 hurricanes have a way of doing that, and Hurricane Andrew was no exception. Yet a strange connection between these two phenomena arose unbidden in my thoughts concerning this matter of hope, along these lines:

In the face of the enormity that was Hurricane Andrew, I did not ask "Why?" I did not seek answers or explanations or even any particular understanding of what was happening that I can recall. I simply stood in awe in the presence of something that seemed beyond comprehension, something that would not have yielded to any feeble efforts I might have made to rationalize or explain it. And perhaps ultimately that is the best we can do in the case of Alzheimer's disease, namely, merely acknowledge the "awe-fulness" of a phenomenon that is clearly beyond our control and even our understanding.

Still, even at the height of Andrew's fury—with the building shaking, the electricity gone, and the water pouring in—I knew that the storm *would* end, that the wind and the rain and, yes, the destruction would stop, and that the sun would shine again. Then would come the task of rebuilding, of working as individuals and as a community to pick up whatever pieces were left, of putting our lives back together and seeking wholeness once more. I could not help but think of the inscription the Allies are said to have found on the wall of a cell when they liberated one of the Nazi concentration camps: "I believe in the sun even when it is not shining. I believe in God even when he seems to be absent." A poem by Emily Dickinson serves to sum up that dark night well:

> "Hope" is the thing with feathers—
> That perches in the soul—
> And sings the tune without the words—
> And never stops—at all—
>
> And sweetest—in the Gale—is heard—
> And sore must be the storm—
> That could abash the little Bird
> That kept so many warm—
>
> I've heard it in the chillest land—
> And on the strangest Sea—
> Yet, never, in Extremity,
> It asked a crumb—of Me.[13]

Yes, in the midst of that storm several years ago, I realized, as David L. Miller so aptly put it in the September 1994 *Lutheran* magazine, that "hope has to do with the presence of God, not the absence of struggle." In fact, from the Christian perspective, it seems that struggle and suffering are necessary for hope. Among many scriptural affirmations, Paul's statement in Romans 5:3–5 is especially clear: We "boast in our sufferings, knowing that suffering produces endurance, and endurance produces character, and character produces hope, and hope does not disappoint us, because God's love has been poured into our hearts through the Holy Spirit that has been given to us."[14] How could Paul see suffering as the basis for hope? Simply because "God proves his love for us in that while we still were sinners Christ died for us" (v. 8) and was raised by God, "the first fruits of those who have died" (1 Cor. 15:20). In short, the resurrection of Christ is the source of the Christian hope that however great the suffering and loss, nothing in "all creation will be able to separate us from the love of God in Christ Jesus our Lord" (Rom. 8:39).

As Paul makes clear, however, and German theologian Jürgen Moltmann (of *Theology of Hope* fame) reaffirms, before the resurrection was the *cross,* which "reveals what is truly evil in the world, . . . the unredeemed condition of the world and its sinking into nothingness."[15] Thus genuine *Christian* hope is not an unrealistic refusal to accept the negativities of life but a realization that even those negativities, even a whole world "groaning in travail together" (Rom. 8:22), even something as vicious and damnable as Alzheimer's disease, cannot prevail against the power and love of God. Martin Luther King Jr., with a wealth of experience of the negativities of this world, aptly expressed the Christian hope when he said, "We must accept finite disappointment, but we must never lose infinite hope."[16] Such an attitude is possible for Christians because in Christ's resurrection, as Moltmann affirms,

> hope is always kindled anew. In him, the future of righteousness and the passing of evil can be hoped for; in him, the future of life and the passing of death can be hoped for; in him, the coming of freedom and the passing of humiliation can be hoped for; in him, the future of . . . true humanity and the passing of inhumanity can be hoped for.[17]

Moltmann is speaking here primarily of social evil. But it is not too far afield to apply his remarks to a natural evil like Alzheimer's disease. In short, as he puts it, "Hope recognizes the power and also the faithfulness of God in this story of the resurrection of the crucified one."[18] In light of *God's* power and faithfulness demonstrated in the resurrection, the poet-statesman Vaclav Havel's magnificent definition of hope takes on even more meaning, especially for those who care for persons with Alzheimer's disease: "Hope is not about believing you can change things. Hope is about believing you make a difference."

It seems fitting to conclude a book that has considered the theological dimensions of Alzheimer's disease with a prayer. Dag Hammarskjöld offers a New Year's prayer in *Markings*[19] that speaks fittingly to the theme of these chapters—memory and hope. The prayer begins with an apt expression of a feeling shared by many persons with Alzheimer's and their caregivers and goes on to address both memory and hope:

—Night is drawing nigh—
For all that has been—Thanks!
To all that shall be—Yes!

NOTES

Chapter 1.
Celebrating the Human Spirit

1. Gardner Murphy, *Historical Introduction to Modern Psychology*, rev. ed. (New York: Harcourt, Brace & Co., 1949), 5.

2. John Calvin, *Institutes of the Christian Religion*, trans. Ford Lewis Battles, ed. John T. McNeill, 2 vols., Library of Christian Classics (Philadelphia: Westminster Press, 1960), 1.15.2.

3. Calvin, *Institutes* 1.15.2.

4. Calvin, *Institutes* 1.15.3.

5. Mary Potter Engel, *John Calvin's Perspectival Anthropology*, American Academy of Religion Academy Series, ed. Susan Thistlethwaite (Atlanta: Scholars Press, 1988), 196.

6. Calvin, *Institutes* 1.15.4.

7. Some individuals seem to have a sudden onset of Alzheimer's disease, but further investigation shows that other emotional or social causes had masked the disease until it was in a more advanced stage. Or a seeming sudden onset can reflect the ability of some people to "cover up" their memory loss until the disease worsens. In other cases, family members who don't live with the impaired individual failed to see the subtle progression of the disease.

8. J. W. Ellor, J. Stettner, and H. Spath, "Ministry with the Confused Elderly," *Journal of Religion and Aging* 4, no. 2 (1987): 21–31.

9. James W. Ellor and Robert B. Coates, "Enhancing the Church as Service Provider to the Elderly through Curriculum Development," *Quarterly Papers on Religion and Aging* 2 (Spring, 1986).

Notes

Chapter 2.
Failing Brain, Faithful God

1. Marylou Tousignant and Bill Miller, "Baby K's Mother Gives Her the Prayer That Many Deny She Has," *Washington Post*, Friday, Oct. 7, 1994, sec. A.

2. "Alzheimer's Disease Fact Sheet," Alzheimer's Association, Chicago, Ill., 1990.

3. Nancy L. Eiesland, *The Disabled God: Toward a Liberatory Theology of Disability* (Nashville: Abingdon Press, 1994), 11.

4. Sharon H. Ringe, "When Women Interpret the Bible," in *The Women's Bible Commentary*, ed. Carol A. Newsom and Sharon H. Ringe (Louisville, Ky.: Westminster/John Knox Press, 1992), 5.

5. Robert Davis, *My Journey into Alzheimer's Disease: A True Story* (Wheaton, Ill.: Tyndale House Publishers, 1989), 108.

6. David Blumenthal, *Facing the Abusing God: A Theology of Protest* (Louisville, Ky.: Westminster/John Knox Press, 1993), 259.

7. Eiesland, *Disabled God*, 71.

8. Ibid., 72.

9. Ibid., 70.

10. Davis, *My Journey into Alzheimer's Disease*, 114.

11. Ibid., 49.

12. Sandy Rovner, "An Alzheimer's Journal," in *Washington Post* Health Section, March 29, 1994, p. 12.

13. Ibid., 15.

14. Eiesland, *Disabled God*, 40.

15. Ibid., 13.

16. Emilie Townes, ed., *A Troubling in My Soul: Womanist Perspectives on Evil and Suffering* (Maryknoll, N.Y.: Orbis Books, 1993), preface.

17. Davis, *My Journey into Alzheimer's Disease*, 108.

18. Jacquelyn Grant, "The Sin of Servanthood and the Deliverance of Discipleship," in Townes, *Troubling in My Soul*, 200.

19. Stephen Sapp, *Full of Years: Aging and the Elderly in the Bible and Today* (Nashville: Abingdon Press,1987), 134–35.

20. John Drakeford, "How Growing Old Looks from Within: A Study of John Wesley's Perception of the Aging Process as Revealed in His Journal's 'Birthday Reflections,'" *Journal of Religion and Aging* 1 (Winter, 1984): 50.

21. Sam Sligar, "A Funeral That Never Ends: Alzheimer's Disease and Pastoral Care," *Journal of Pastoral Care* 41 (December, 1987): 344.

22. Judah Ronch, *Alzheimer's Disease: A Guide for Those Who Help Others* (New York: Continuum, 1989), 182.

23. T. Adler, "Alzheimer's Causes Unique Cell Death," *Science News* 146 (Sept. 24, 1994): 198.

24. Ronch, *Alzheimer's Disease,* 39.

25. Davis, *My Journey into Alzheimer's Disease,* 140.

26. Ronch, *Alzheimer's Disease,* 40.

27. Davis, *My Journey into Alzheimer's Disease,* 102.

28. Rovner, "Alzheimer's Journal," 12.

29. Molly Tully and Mary Ann Blotzer, *Surviving Today and Revising Tomorrow: Caregiving Strategies for the Alzheimer's Spouse* (Washington, D.C.: Alzheimer's Disease and Related Disorders Association of Greater Washington, 1993), 13.

30. Ibid., 15.

31. Davis, *My Journey into Alzheimer's Disease,* 113.

32. Bruce Birch, "Biblical Faith and the Loss of Children," *Christian Century,* Oct. 26,1983, 966.

33. Terence Fretheim, *The Suffering of God* (Philadelphia: Fortress Press, 1984), 128.

34. Abraham Joshua Heschel, *The Prophets: An Introduction,* vol. 1 (New York: Harper & Row, 1962), 113.

35. Brian Wren, *What Language Shall I Borrow? God-Talk in Worship: A Male Response to Feminist Theology* (New York: Crossroad, 1991), 115.

36. Fretheim, *Suffering of God,* 68.

37. Ibid., 69.

38. Davis, *My Journey into Alzheimer's Disease,* 59.

39. Ibid., 110.

40. Ibid., 48, 47.

Chapter 3.
Memory: The Community Looks Backward

1. C. J. Dippel and G. de Santillana quoted by Jürgen Moltmann in "Theology in the World of Modern Science," in *Hope and Planning,* trans. Margaret Clarkson (New York: Harper & Row, 1971), 218;

from E. Wolf, "Theologie und Naturwissenschaft," *Monatsschrift für Pastoraltheologie* 54 (1965): 331.

2. Oliver Sacks, *The Man Who Mistook His Wife for a Hat and Other Clinical Tales* (New York: Harper & Row, 1985), 23 (no citation is given for Buñuel's memoirs).

3. Ibid., 34.

4. Gilbert Meilaender, *"Terra es animata:* On Having a Life," *Hastings Center Report* 23 (July/August, 1993): 25–32. I am indebted to this essay for a number of the points that follow.

5. Augustine, *City of God,* trans. Henry Bettenson, ed. David Knowles (New York: Penguin Books, 1972), 937.

6. Paul Ramsey, *Fabricated Man: The Ethics of Genetic Control* (New Haven, Conn.: Yale University Press, 1970), 87.

7. *The Philosophical Works of Descartes,* trans. Elizabeth S. Haldane and G. R. T. Ross, 2 vols. (Cambridge: Cambridge University Press, 1931). Concise, helpful summaries of the philosophy of Descartes may be found in Frederick Copleston, *A History of Philosophy,* vol. 4: *Descartes to Leibniz* (Garden City, N.Y.: Image Books, 1960), 74–160; and in E. A. Burtt, *The Metaphysical Foundations of Modern Science,* rev. ed. (Garden City, N.Y.: Doubleday & Co., 1954), 105–24.

8. Meilaender, *"Terra es animata,"* 29.

9. Reinhold Niebuhr, "A View of Life from the Sidelines," *Christian Century,* Dec. 19–26, 1984, 1197.

10. Meilaender, *"Terra es animata,"* 32.

11. H. Wheeler Robinson, *Corporate Personality in Ancient Israel* (Philadelphia: Fortress Press, 1964). This view contends that in ancient Israel, an individual such as a head of a clan or authority figure represents or "sums up" the whole community in that person's self. Also, the actions of one person (such as the sin of Achan in Joshua 7) have consequences and effects for the whole community.

12. In chapter 5 of this book, Denise Dombkowski Hopkins offers some helpful insights along these same lines (see especially pp. 85–87). In particular, she quotes Judah Ronch's observation that "patients can be made to feel less anxious if they are part of something more continuous than their own fragmented existence" (*Alzheimer's Disease,* 30). She goes on to affirm that "a resurrection theology for dementia should include assurances that patients remain one with the

whole body of Christ." She also echoes the point made in this chapter by citing Glenn Weaver's insightful reminder that "memory is a social experience" ("Senile Dementia and a Resurrection Theology," *Theology Today* 42 [January, 1986]: 44).

13. By way of partial illustration of the point being made in this section, a perhaps surprising source for theological insight may be cited—Billy Joel. His recent compact disc *River of Dreams* contains a song he wrote for his daughter titled "Lullabye (Goodnight, My Angel)," which illustrates quite well the idea that it is in memory (i.e., in *others'* remembering) that individuals are kept "alive" after they die (or lose their own memory?). Ideas contained in popular lullabyes of course fall far short of the Christian hope for a continued personal existence after death. But the song expresses the normal human desire for continued existence in at least some sense with those whom one has known and loved and vice versa.

Chapter 4.
Love, Wisdom, and Justice: Transcendent Caring

1. Paul Tillich, *Ethical Principles of Moral Action; Being and Doing: Paul Tillich as Ethicist*, ed. John J. Carey (Macon, Ga.: Mercer University Press, 1987), 216.

2. Ibid., 212.

3. See ibid., 205–17.

4. John Calvin, *Commentaries on The Four Last Books of Moses Arranged in the Form of a Harmony*, trans. Charles William Bingham (Grand Rapids: Baker Book House, 1993), 7.

5. Ibid.

6. Ibid., 8.

7. Ibid.

8. Ibid., 8–9.

9. Norman Linzer, "The Obligations of Adult Children to Aged Parents: A View from Jewish Tradition," *Journal of Aging and Judaism* 1 (1986): 34–48.

10. See Gibson Winter, *Love and Conflict* (Garden City, N.Y.: Doubleday & Co., 1958), 159–81.

11. Ibid., 160.

12. Ibid., 170.

13. Ibid.

Chapter 5.
Failing Brain, Faithful Community

1. Sandy Burgener, "Caregiver Religiosity and Well-Being in Dealing with Alzheimer's Dementia," *Journal of Religion and Health* 33 (Summer, 1994): 187.

2. Cited in Ronch, *Alzheimer's Disease.*

3. Davis, *My Journey into Alzheimer's Disease,* 18.

4. Cited in Rovner, "Alzheimer's Journal," 15.

5. Ronch, *Alzheimer's Disease,* 19, 32, 22.

6. Ibid., 31.

7. Davis, *My Journey into Alzheimer's Disease,* 86.

8. Ibid., 114.

9. Ronch, *Alzheimer's Disease,* 12.

10. Davis, *My Journey into Alzheimer's Disease,* 100.

11. Ibid., 101.

12. Rebecca Chopp, "Writing Women's Lives," *Memphis Theological Seminary Journal* 29 (Spring, 1991): 10.

13. Chopp observes that even in feminist theology, "a certain romanticization of the body through claims of embodiment inscribes the normal body as the perfect body," in Eiesland, *Disabled God,* 10.

14. Davis, *My Journey into Alzheimer's Disease,* 101.

15. Ronch, *Alzheimer's Disease,* 37.

16. Roland Murphy, "The Faith of the Psalmist," *Interpretation* 34 (1980): 236.

17. Davis, *My Journey into Alzheimer's Disease,* 20, 48.

18. Ibid., 140.

19. Harold Kushner, *When Bad Things Happen to Good People* (New York: Schocken Books, 1981), 88.

20. Daniel Simundson, *Faith under Fire: Biblical Interpretations of Suffering* (Minneapolis: Augsburg, 1980), 97.

21. Wren, *What Language Shall I Borrow?* 115.

22. Nancy Eiesland argues for changing the symbol of Christ from the Suffering Servant or conquering Lord, toward a formula of Christ

as disabled God, at least for particular people in particular situations of pain. Hers is a "contextual Christology" focusing on Luke 24:36–39, for "in presenting his impaired hands and feet to his startled friends, the resurrected Jesus is revealed as the disabled God" (p. 100). This is an honest body experiencing life as a mixed blessing. She wants to give up belief in "an all-powerful God who could heal if He would" (p. 105).

23. See Denise Dombkowski Hopkins, *Journey through the Psalms: A Path to Wholeness* (New York: United Church Press, 1990), 47.

24. "The Prozac Society," *Washington Post*, Style Section, Dec. 5, 1993, sec. C.

25. Davis, *My Journey into Alzheimer's Disease*, 103.

26. Arden Barden, "Toward New Directions for Ministry in Aging: An Overview of Issues and Concepts," in *The Role of the Church in Aging: Implications for Policy and Action*, ed. Michael Hendrickson (New York: Hayworth Press, 1986), 140.

27. Ronch, *Alzheimer's Disease*, 29.

28. Barden, "Toward New Directions," 140.

29. Ronch, *Alzheimer's Disease*, 26.

30. Rovner, "Alzheimer's Journal," 15.

31. Davis, *My Journey into Alzheimer's Disease*, 48, 96.

32. Ibid., 125.

33. Hopkins, *Journey through the Psalms*, 83.

34. Walter Brueggemann, *The Message of the Psalms* (Minneapolis: Augsburg, 1984), 55.

35. Darrell Fasching, "Faith and Ethics after the Holocaust: What Christians Can Learn from the Jewish Narrative Tradition of *Hutzpah*," *Journal of Ecumenical Studies* 27 (Summer, 1990): 455.

36. See Samuel E. Balentine, *Prayer in the Hebrew Bible: The Drama of Divine-Human Dialogue* (Minneapolis: Fortress Press, 1993).

37. Ronch, *Alzheimer's Disease*, 67.

38. Cited in Hopkins, *Journey through the Psalms*, 91.

39. Carol A. Newsom, "Job," in *The Women's Bible Commentary*, ed. Carol A. Newson and Sharon H. Ringe (Louisville, Ky.: Westminster/John Knox Press, 1992), 132.

40. Ronch, *Alzheimer's Disease*, 64.

41. Davis, *My Journey into Alzheimer's Disease*, 110.

42. Ronch, *Alzheimer's Disease*, 30.

43. I am indebted to my husband, David Hopkins, for this idea.

44. Balentine, *Prayer in the Hebrew Bible,* 290.

45. Ibid., 291.

46. Glenn Weaver, "Senile Dementia and a Resurrection Theology," *Theology Today* 42 (January, 1986): 44.

47. Davis, *My Journey into Alzheimer's Disease,* 18.

48. Bruce Birch, "Biblical Faith and the Loss of Children," *Christian Century* (Oct. 26, 1983): 967.

49. Perry LeFevre, "Toward a Theology of Aging," *Chicago Theological Seminary Register* 74 (Fall, 1984): 10.

50. Ibid., 11.

51. Davis, *My Journey into Alzheimer's Disease,* 107.

Chapter 6.
Hope: The Community Looks Forward

1. Personal communication. Eisdorfer is also the source of a delightful paraphrase of the well-known remark about war and generals: "Aging is too important to be left to the gerontologists."

2. David Keck, *Forgetting Whose We Are: Alzheimer's Disease and the Love of God* (Nashville: Abingdon Press, 1996), 38. This thoughtful book, which explores many of the issues discussed in chapters 3 and 6 of the present volume in much greater depth than was possible here, rewards the efforts required to read it.

3. Mary Potter Engel, *John Calvin's Perspectival Anthropology,* American Academy of Religion Academy Series, ed. Susan Thistlethwaite (Atlanta: Scholars Press, 1988), 189.

4. John Calvin, *Institutes of the Christian Religion,* trans. Ford Lewis Battles, ed. John T. McNeill, 2 vols., Library of Christian Classics (Philadelphia: Westminster Press, 1960), 3.7.1.

5. One cannot help but think in this context of Paul's exposition in 1 Cor. 1:18–31 of the standards that God uses to determine the worth of individuals. God's criteria are very different from those that the world brings to bear to judge the value of human beings. For a fuller discussion of this point, see Sapp, *Full of Years,* 147–49.

6. Thomas F. Torrance, *Calvin's Doctrine of Man* (Grand Rapids: Wm. B. Eerdmans Publishing Co., 1957; Westport, Conn.: Greenwood Press, 1977), 61.

7. It is not only from the Christian perspective that this view is problematic. At the White House Conference on Aging in 1971, Rabbi Abraham Heschel affirmed,

> It takes three things to attain a sense of significant being:
> God
> A soul
> A moment
> These three are always with us.
> Just to be is a blessing,
> Just to live is holy.

8. John Calvin, *Sermons on Job* 14:16f., quoted in Torrance, *Calvin's Doctrine of Man*, 74.

9. This discussion calls to mind a comment the well-known Protestant ethicist Stanley Hauerwas once made at a conference, a remark significantly out of step with the dominant contemporary American ethos (as are most of Hauerwas's statements): "There is no assertion more chilling in modernity than 'I don't want to be a burden to my children.' What else are children for?"

10. John H. Leith, *John Calvin's Doctrine of the Christian Life* (Louisville, Ky.: Westminster/John Knox Press, 1989), 167, 215.

11. *Corpus Reformatorum: Joannis Calvini Opera Quae Supersunt Omnia*, ed. Guilielmus Baum, Eduardus Cunitz, and Eduardus Reuss (Brunswick: C. A. Schwetschke et Filium, 1863–1897), 49:505; hereafter cited as *CR*. This and subsequent references to this source come from citations in Leith, *John Calvin's Doctrine of the Christian Life*.

12. In *Institutes* 4.1.2, Calvin states explicitly, "It is as if one said that the saints are gathered into the society of Christ on the principle that whatever benefits God confers upon them, they should in turn share with one another"; and again, "If truly convinced that God is the common Father of all and Christ the common Head, being united in brotherly love, they cannot but share their benefits with one another." In one of his sermons, Calvin asserts that "our Lord has made us stewards of his goods which He has put into our hands, not to the end that every one of us should devour them by himself alone, but that we should communicate them to such as have need of them."

Notes

Sermons from Job, trans. Leroy Nixon (Grand Rapids: Baker Book House, 1952), 200.

13. *The Complete Poems of Emily Dickinson,* ed. Thomas H. Johnson (Boston: Little, Brown & Co., 1960), 116. Used with permission of Little, Brown and Company.

14. The author of 1 Peter, writing to Christians in Asia Minor who were suffering because of their conversion, reflects the same perspective: "You know that your brothers and sisters in all the world are undergoing the same kinds of suffering. And after you have suffered for a little while, the God of all grace, who has called you to eternal glory in Christ, will himself restore, support, strengthen, and establish you" (5:9–10). It is not very difficult to see the applicability of this statement to persons with Alzheimer's disease and their caregivers, surely a source of real hope for them.

15. Moltmann, *Hope and Planning,* 194.

16. Quoted by Martin E. Marty from a Christmas card, *Context* 27 (May 1, 1995): 6.

17. Moltmann, *Hope and Planning,* 194–5.

18. Ibid., 183.

19. Dag Hammarskjöld, *Markings,* trans. Leif Sjoberg and W. H. Auden (London: Faber & Faber, 1964), 87.

INDEX OF SCRIPTURE

Index of Scripture

INDEX OF SUBJECTS

Index of Subjects